WOOD ON WHEELS

WOOD ON WHEELS

Making Toys That Rock & Roll, Wiggle & Shake

Kevin McGuire

A Sterling/Lark Book

Sterling Publishing Co., Inc. New York

Editor: Chris Rich
Art Director: Chris Bryant
Production: Chris Bryant and Elaine Thompson
Illustrations: Don Osby
Photography: Evan Bracken

Library of Congress Cataloging-in-Publication Data
McGuire, Kevin.
    Wood on wheels : making toys that rock & roll, wiggle & shake /
by Kevin McGuire
      p. cm.
    "A Sterling/Lark book."
    Includes index.
    ISBN 0-8069-1286-3
    1. Wooden toy making. 2. Mechanical toys. I. Title.
TT174.5.W6M43   1995
745.592--dc20   94-37136
                                      CIP

10 9 8 7 6 5 4 3 2 1

A Sterling/Lark Book

Published in 1995 by Sterling Publishing Company, Inc.
  387 Park Avenue South, New York, N.Y. 10016

Produced by Altamont Press, Inc.
  50 College Street, Asheville, NC 28801

© 1995 by Kevin McGuire

Distributed in Canada by Sterling Publishing
  c/o Canadian Manda Group, One Atlantic Avenue,
  Suite 105, Toronto, Ontario, Canada M6K 3E7
Distributed in Great Britain and Europe by Cassell PLC,
  Villiers House, 41/47 Strand, London WC2N 5JE, England
Distributed in Australia by Capricorn Link (Australia) Pty Ltd.,
  P.O. Box 6651, Baulkham Hills, Business Centre, NSW 2153, Australia

Every effort has been made to ensure that all information in this book is
accurate. However, due to differing conditions, tools, and individual skills,
the publisher cannot be responsible for any injuries, losses, or other
damages which may result from the use of the information in this book.

Printed in Hong Kong by Oceanic Graphic Printing.

Sterling ISBN 0-8069-1286-3

TABLE OF CONTENTS

• • • •

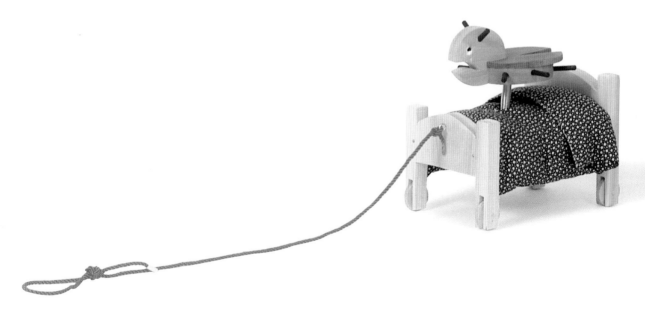

introduction

KIDS IN MOTION

· · · ·

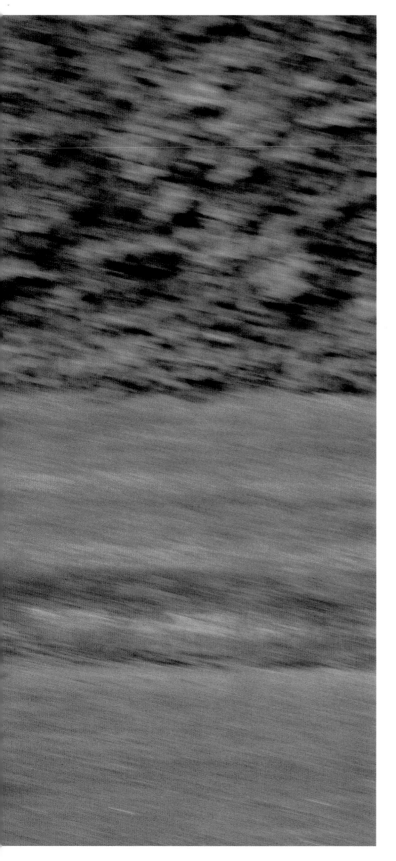

No one enjoys the excitement of high-speed, naturally powered travel quite like kids. In fact, those blurs that just passed by may well have been youngsters on their way to meet other blurs in the neighborhood, and most of them were probably towing or toting a rolling or rocking thingamajig of some sort, just for the fun of it.

This book is a builder's guide to the amazing possibilities of homemade motion toys. Whether you're an experienced woodworker grazing for creative building ideas or a novice getting ready to make your first project, you'll find plenty of riding, rolling, and rocking thrills in the pages to come. And your kids will love you for your efforts!

The history of motion toys is a complex and fascinating one that stretches back beyond recorded memory and across all cultures. From the votive toys of ancient Egypt to the clockwork-like wooden motion toys of Europe and beyond, a bewildering variety of styles and mechanisms has flourished throughout the years. You want to build, but where do you begin?

Wood on Wheels is designed to answer your most basic questions, to steer you through the maze, and to get the projects built and where they belong—into the hands of a happy child. The introduction, "Kids in Motion," starts with basic information on sharing shop time with your kids, choosing projects that are age appropriate, and monitoring for play safety. Spending a little time with these opening pages will help you decide which projects your kids will enjoy most. The next section, "Tools, Techniques, and Materials," contains the nuts and bolts—the "what" and "how" of building motion toys. Here you'll find descriptions of efficient shop design, a wide variety of tools and materials, and the techniques unique to building the projects included in this book.

In the third section, "The Projects," you'll discover a movable feast of playthings on-the-go, divided into three groups. "Small Wonders" features push and pull toys, each of which displays a different type of movement or appearance. "Rock and Roll!" offers larger projects that have wheels, rockers, or runners. "Movin' On" is a dreamscape of specialty toys, display toys, and accessories such as traffic signs and a gas pump to make your kids' playtime even more fun. Every project includes complete lists of materials, hardware and supplies, and recommended tools, as well as diagrams, photos, and clear, step-by-step instructions.

This book was written with real respect for the toymakers of old, who have given children some outrageously good times throughout the years. Take the time to build safely, have fun, and welcome to *Wood on Wheels*!

WORKING WITH YOUR KIDS

Involving young people in selecting and building play projects provides a unique opportunity for introducing them to the joys of woodworking. Your children's natural curiosity about assembling seemingly unrelated parts into a working whole will be enhanced by their eager anticipation of the completed playthings. Their enthusiasm, however, will need to be tempered by plenty of direction.

By all means let your kids select their projects; the ones they find interesting are the ones they're most likely to use. Before they choose projects from this book, however, let them know which ones might be inappropriate for their age group (see the "Average Developmental List" on page 13).

Introduce your kids to the shop as a place that requires the same sort of organization, effort, and upkeep as any other room in the house. When children begin with this understanding, the few minutes that they'll have to spend on daily preparation, maintenance, and cleanup will seem less like onerous chores and more like necessary parts of the building process. Let them know that well-built playthings are the results not just of sawing and hammering but of stowing wood scraps and oiling tools as well.

Using even basic tools can be a frustrating experience for young people because it involves new and unfamiliar materials and complex eye-hand coordination skills. The best teaching approach is a gradual one that emphasizes the step-by-step nature of each process. Kids' know-how, strength, and endurance are very different from your own; lend them a steady hand when their own smaller hands tire. Get your kids trade-quality tools that match their body and hand sizes and keep these tools well maintained. Also provide your kids with a work surface of appropriate height.

Safety rules for young woodworkers are identical to those for adults. Remember, though, that kids often lack judgement, which is, after all, a product of experience. Always demonstrate the use of a specific tool or material first; then let your child experiment, intervening only when you see unsafe practices or exhaustion setting in. Within safe limits, give your kids the chance to make mistakes and to learn valuable lessons from them.

Try "modeling" (building the same project simultaneously) so that your kids can observe a mirror image of their efforts and have something to strive towards. This technique combines collaborative building and an opportunity for children to work on projects that are truly their own. When the projects are completed, you can celebrate together!

WILL THEY USE IT?

Most adults have had the distressing experience of surprising kids with a toy, only to discover that same toy growing cobwebs later on. Unless the motion toys that you select are age appropriate, your kids may not enjoy them for long.

Kids need playthings that involve the whole range of their developing faculties. Toys should amuse, of course, but should also engage and challenge children's imaginative and problem-solving skills, their need for shared play, and their motor-development levels. Motion toys can meet all these requirements; an examination of the projects in this book will give you a sense of what each one has to offer.

The list that follows, in which you'll find an average developmental level provided for every project, will offer some project-selection guidance. You're the best judge of your child's developmental needs, however; if the list and your own instincts don't coincide, talk the matter over with the experts—the kids themselves—or visit your local library for information on how play functions in the development of children. Still stumped? Select projects at the upper end of what you view as your child's needs; your child won't be getting any younger!

AVERAGE DEVELOPMENTAL LIST

Project	Age	Project	Age
Barge	2-4	Puzzle Truck	3-6
Bed Bug	1-3	Ramblin' Rabbit	1-3
Bike Rack	4 and up	Rattle Mower	1-5
Bob's Sled	1-3	Road Signs	3 and up
Classic Hobbyhorse	3-6	Rollerboy	1-3
Fred Flounder	1-3	Rope Walker	3 and up
Fun Roller	4-6	Scooter	4-6
Garden Cart	3-6	Shopping Cart	3-6
Gas Pump	3 and up	Space Cruiser	4-10
Hoppytoad Rocker	2-4	Spool Tractor	4 and up
Hungry Gator	2-3	Squeegee	3 and up
Little Red Wagon	3-6	Trundle Block Wagon	1-3
Luge	4-6	Tuggy Boat	2-4
Minicycle	1-2	Turtle Dove	1-3
Oilcan	3 and up	Twig Dragon	1-3
Plato the Platypus	3-6	Western Pony	2 and up
Prizewinner	3 and up	Wind Roller	6 and up
Push Goat	1-2		

PLAY SAFETY

Monitoring child's play for safety is second nature for concerned adults, but the use of playthings that rock, roll, and slide suggests a need for extra attention to ensure that everyone has fun and no one gets hurt. You know your children best and can best decide which projects they can handle and use safely, but keep the following points in mind.

- *All shop-built projects should be checked for safe construction before they go to their young owners. Make sure that sharp edges are rounded, hardware is properly installed, and parts are assembled correctly from high-quality materials.*

- *Under no circumstances should these projects be disassembled by children. Loose parts are a special danger for youngsters, so promptly repair any toys that are damaged.*

- *Finishes should be child-safe, and playthings for children under three years of age should contain no loose parts that might cause choking.*

- *Playing with motion toys on hills or in high-traffic areas is a good recipe for disaster and should be unacceptable. The use of riding toys in particular should be monitored by adults, and inappropriate use (more riders than a given toy can handle, for example) should be discouraged.*

- *Children on rolling toys should never, under any circumstances, be towed behind moving vehicles!*

Motion toys provide kids with a wonderful sense of freedom, and riding toys offer the exhilarating extra ingredient of speedy travel. Teach your youngsters that creative play can be safe play, too, and they'll have a rolling good time with their new playthings.

TOOLS
TECHNIQUES
and
MATERIALS
••••

Tools and Techniques

●●●●

Building toys that rock, wiggle, and roll doesn't require exotic woods, complicated hardware, or fancy tools. The playful spirit of the projects in this book is expressed through a no-nonsense combination of sound design, sturdy materials, and selected tools maintained in top condition. Basic construction and a short tools list let the builder enjoy the process as much as the kids enjoy the results.

Whatever your level of experience, the following pages bear careful attention. Taking a few minutes now to review the information provided about work-space efficiency, recommended tools and materials, and shop techniques will ensure a better understanding later on of how to involve your children in the building process and will help you understand how the projects are put together. Do keep in mind that the scope of this book is necessarily limited and that there are as many ways to use an adjustable square or a paring chisel as there are woodworkers who use them.

If you're a newcomer to woodworking, purchase tools as you need them and invest in high-quality tools only. Inexpensive tools don't work well and don't last long, so buy the best that you can afford.

A SAFE AND EFFICIENT SHOP

Whether your work space is a humble bench set up in the corner of your garage or a custom-designed shop filled with all the latest in high-technology equipment, basic requirements for safety and efficiency are the same. The more time you spend at your workbench, the more you'll come to appreciate a shop environment that is orderly, safe, and productive.

Every shop's electrical, ventilation, and fire-suppression systems should meet all code requirements and be reliable at all times. Unless you're competent at wiring, have a licensed electrician install any necessary additions to your shop's electrical system. Even simple upgrades such as light fixtures and drop cords can put a strain on your present wiring, so get professional assistance before you make any changes.

Check your grounded extension cords and power tools regularly for wear and avoid using power tools outdoors in damp weather. For safety's sake, lighting and power installations should fully meet your workshop needs.

To keep sawdust and noxious fumes at a safe level, install appropriate exhaust and ventilation equipment at the source of the problem. This can be costly but is a good investment when weighed against your continued good health. Ventilation specialists can help you design a basic system. Paper dust masks aren't effective when it comes to airborne particulates and simply don't work to protect you against fumes. Invest in a high-quality respirator that is rated to be effective protection against the hazards in your shop—and wear it regularly.

Approved safety glasses and hearing protectors aren't especially attractive, but they're an absolute necessity where safety and health are concerned. Purchase them—and wear them!

Fire safety begins with maintaining a shop that is free of wood scraps and solvent-soaked rags. Your local fire department can offer suggestions on safe storage and disposal of workshop materials. Avoid sources of heat and flame when using flammable products. Keep a fire extinguisher on hand, have it checked regularly, and know how to use it.

Smaller shops in particular will benefit from a floor plan that maximizes available space. If possible, store your accumulated materials in a location adjacent to, rather than within, your work space; this will keep your work area free of clutter and will let you focus on the project at hand. Where space permits, overhead storage is an excellent method for stacking stock that must remain flat, such as lumber and plywood. Suspend a stout rack from the ceiling or secure it to a wall.

Locate tools where you can retrieve them with as little travel as possible and put them neatly away as your work day progresses. Almost any sort of multitiered cubby or cabinet with drawers will serve nicely for tool storage, as long as it isn't so deep that it invites lost tools. To protect tools from moisture and weather extremes, maintain even temperatures and very low humidity in your work space.

Once established, poor shop habits are hard to break. Because they often start with a shop layout that creates problems rather than solves them, it's a good idea to set up the elements of your shop in a way that will encourage regular cleanup and adequate tool maintenance and that will create as little wear and tear on your hardworking body as possible.

WORK SUPPORTS

Work supports are tools, too, and shop-built ones can be customized to meet your particular needs.

SAWHORSES

You'll need a pair of sturdy sawhorses as a support for cutting out many of the project parts and for sanding and finishing work as well. If setting these up outdoors (just outside your workshop) won't create noise problems for your neighbors, then by all means do so; working outdoors provides plenty of fresh air that helps disperse fine sawdust particles.

Your sawhorses should be constructed of sturdy material and should have no hardware installed within 3" of their top surfaces. If they're hip-height, they'll help avoid strain on your back.

WORKBENCH

This indispensable tool is available in a variety of shapes and sizes and can cost the equivalent of a deli sandwich or a catered party. Whether you build or buy it, your workbench should be assembled from substantial timbers that are glued or bolted together for a strong, vibration-free work surface. Cross-bracing will reduce *racking*, the lateral shifting under load that is every woodworker's nightmare.

These days, "Euro-style" benches come equipped with more options than late-model cars. Perhaps the most useful are the *tool trough*, a broad recess in the work surface that keeps frequently used tools within easy reach, and a *bench vise*, which puts a firm grip on your work. *Dogs*—small wooden or metal stops that fit in bench-top holes—work in tandem with a vise to secure oddly shaped, unwieldy stock.

If you build your own bench, begin by purchasing one or two bench vises of a weight and quality suited to your intended work and design the bench around the vises. Workbenches and components are available at shops specializing in woodworking supplies and are also advertised in the trade journals found at larger libraries. They're typically built so that the top is approximately the same height as the user's hips.

ASSEMBLY BENCH

This shop-built companion to the workbench is simply a low, wide support that greatly reduces strain on your upper body during assembly time. (A workbench is too high to be suitable for assembling larger parts.) Make your assembly bench about 30" high, depending upon your height, and as long and wide as your floor space will permit.

LAYOUT TOOLS

Well-built motion toys begin with exact layouts. The following tools are basic for making these.

NO. 2 PENCILS
Lay in a good supply and keep them sharp.

TAPE MEASURE
Next to your pencil, a 16'-long tape measure will be your most frequently used tool. Better-quality tape measures allow tape replacement without replacing the metal case. Inexpensive tapes are a waste of your money, as they wear out much faster than better ones, resulting in inaccurate measurements and poorly fitted parts. Accurate measurement depends upon holding this tool securely in position, neither stretching the tape nor allowing slack along its length.

TRY SQUARE
This small 90-degree square is useful for squaring across boards before sawing and for checking 90-degree angle joints. Purchase one with a *beam* (or blade) at least 8" long. When you use this tool, always keep its handle tight against the stock. On very wide boards, first square from one edge of the board and then continue the squared line from the opposite edge—or use a framing square instead.

COMBINATION SQUARE
This metal tool has an adjustable beam that's held at 90 degrees to its handle. Useful for laying out *rip cuts* (cuts along the length of stock), a combination square can also be used to square across wider stock such as 1 x 8s or 1 x 10s.

FRAMING SQUARE
Grandmother to the try square, this large 90-degree layout tool will help you create layouts that stretch to the midpoint of a 4' x 8' piece of plywood. A steel framing square is more durable than an aluminum one.

ADJUSTABLE PROTRACTOR
This tool's degree markings and adjustable indicator make it easy to establish angled layouts and transfer angles from existing saw cuts to new stock. If your tool supplier doesn't carry adjustable protractors, contact an engineering-supply company or check the catalogues.

STRAIGHTEDGE
This metal ruler allows you to mark off measurements as you scribe a straight line. A 24"-long straightedge is helpful, but a 36"-long one is even better.

COMPASS
Lightweight versions such as those found on school-supply display racks are fine for the occasional circles you'll be scribing for these projects.

CENTER FINDER
This specialty tool makes locating a dowel's true center a snap. Check the catalogues for this unusual and inexpensive addition to your shop.

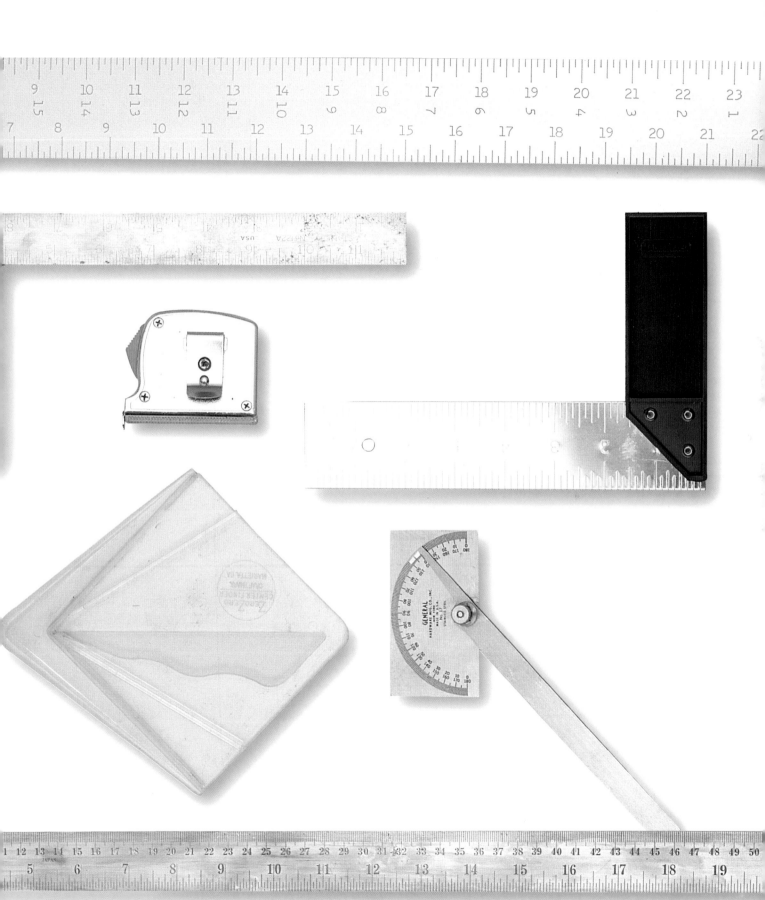

HAND TOOLS

Though you can't build these projects without the basic hand tools described in the next few pages, there's no point to purchasing them all at once. Build a collection as you can afford it, borrowing tools in the interim.

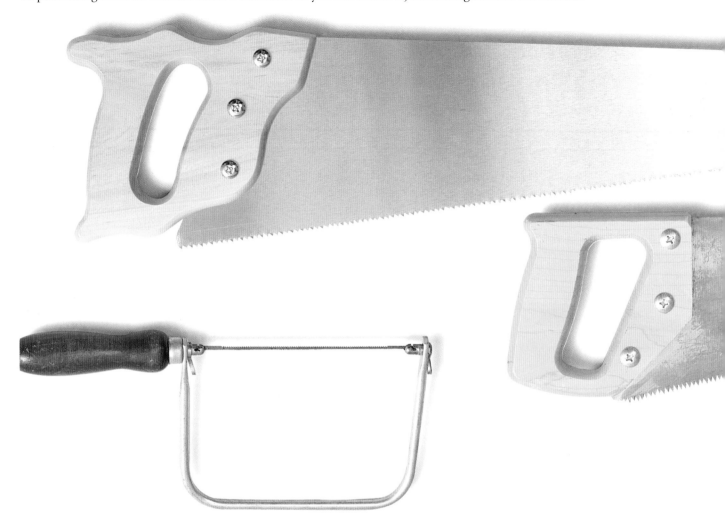

Saws and Miter Box

You'll need four saws for these projects, as well as a sawyer's tool known as a miter box.

PANEL SAW

The *crosscut panel saw* (shown at the top of the photo) is used to cut thick or wide stock across the wood grain. (A *ripsaw* cuts along the grain.) For general work, use a blade with eight teeth per inch.

When it's accurately started, a saw cut rarely wanders from the layout line. To start a cut without chipping the wood, first make a shallow groove by drawing the saw teeth backwards several times at the layout line. Then continue cutting back and forth, using your body and shoulder to power the saw and maintaining your shoulder, elbow, and hand in alignment. For maximum efficiency, saw slowly and deliberately.

BACKSAW

This small saw is used to make shallow, straight cuts in all stock and is especially effective at cutting dowels when used in conjunction with a miter box. Typical backsaws have fine teeth, a rectangular blade, and a thick back piece for added stability. Hold this saw just as you would hold a panel saw, but don't exert as much force when you use it.

The saw that was used to build these projects (shown just below the crosscut saw in the photo) is actually a variant that is smaller than a panel saw and larger than the typical backsaw; it's used in identical fashion to the backsaw. Either a backsaw or this variant will do for the projects in this book.

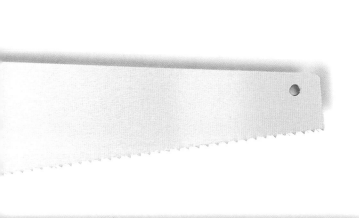

MITER BOX

Designed to help take the guesswork out of making square cuts in small stock, this tool is easily built in your shop. Cut to size three 3/4" x 3-1/2" x 12" pieces of lumber. Using 6d finishing nails, fasten two of the pieces to the third piece to create an assembly that is C-shaped in cross-section. Square across the middle of the two outside pieces of the assembly, aligning the squared lines exactly across it. Then simultaneously saw matching slots along the two lines, stopping the cut when you reach the middle (or base) piece. For your miter box to function properly, the two cuts must be exactly perpendicular to the base and aligned squarely across the assembly. Sand the completed miter box well.

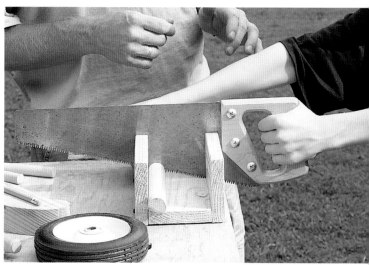

COPING SAW

This saw's U-shaped frame and thin, flexible blade make it easy to saw curved cuts in thinner stock; its thin blade can cut tighter circles than a power jigsaw. Rotating the blade in the frame's twin pin holders allows you to work around protruding edges of stock.

To make interior cutouts, first use a drill to bore a starter hole in an inside corner of the layout. Then loosen the coping-saw blade, slip it through the hole, and retighten the blade in its frame.

The coping saw is generally used with the handle held in a vertical position and below the frame. For accurate results, make sure the stock that's being cut is well secured at all times. Keep a package of extra blades on hand.

FRETSAW

Perfect for fine, curving cuts in balsa wood and other fragile stock, the fretsaw resembles a miniature coping saw, right down to the ultra-fine teeth. The frames on most fretsaws adjust for different blade lengths and even for snapped blade remnants. Gentle pressure is a must when sawing.

In a pinch, the coping saw can do much of the work of the fretsaw.

Rasps

For shaping rough wood surfaces, rasps are real work-horses. They're available in many shapes and sizes for various smoothing jobs.

FLAT, HALF-ROUND, AND ROUND RASPS

These time-savers remove wood in a hurry, smoothing rough stock in preparation for sanding. Most rasps' serrated teeth remove material on the forward stroke only. Ask your supplier for a *file card*, which will increase your rasps' effectiveness by removing accumulated wood particles from their serrations. Choose rasps that have shapes appropriate for the work you're doing.

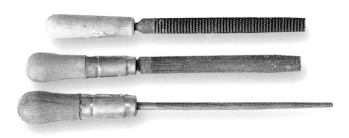

Planes

These smoothers remove tool marks left by saws and rasps to provide a near perfect surface on your flat stock. For information on sharpening these and other edged tools, see "Sharpening Basics" on the opposite page.

LOW-ANGLE BLOCK PLANE

Of the numerous planes available, this beauty is the most useful for our projects. Palm sized and comfortably weighted, it simplifies trimming the rough spots left by saw teeth along the edges of stock, and the low angle of the plane iron's cutting edge makes smoothing end grain and knotty lumber possible.

Keep the cutting edge razor sharp and the mechanism well adjusted. Using the low-angle block plane is a simple matter of applying firm, even pressure as you slide the tool along the wood's surface. If you aren't satisfied with the plane's performance and you know that the edge of the iron is sharp, the plane probably needs adjustment.

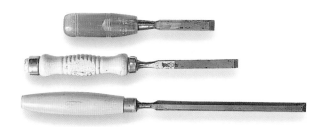

Chisels

A bewildering variety of these chippers and choppers can be purchased, but only a few are really necessary for the projects in this book.

CARPENTER'S CHISEL

Short in handle and shank, this chisel's plastic-and-steel construction is virtually bombproof. Although its small pattern makes it less easy to control than larger models, the carpenter's chisel is ideal for working in confined spaces. Purchase a set of at least four sizes.

FIRMER CHISEL

This large-patterned chisel has a substantial wooden handle and a long, thick shank that's rectangular in cross-section. A metal ring protects the handle end against "mushrooming" when it is struck. The heft of the firmer chisel makes it a favorite for serious wood removal, but a complete set can be costly. One alternative is to purchase individual chisels as you need them.

PARING CHISEL

Also called a *patternmaker's chisel*, this tool is powered by directing force from the shoulder through the arm to the hand; the handle is never struck with a mallet. Once a joint is shaped, the paring chisel is effective in removing thin sections of wood for final fitting. Try out one of the smaller sizes, and you'll want to build a complete set.

sharpening basics

Keeping chisels, plane irons, and other edged tools sharp is neither difficult nor time-consuming, but it does require an understanding of basic sharpening tools and techniques. The tips offered here will keep your tools cutting cleanly.

The "edge" of most edged tools is actually the beveled portion of the working tip—a portion that requires regular touch-ups. The bevel's angle is crucial to the type of work done by a particular tool, so familiarize yourself with the bevels of your tools, using a protractor as a guide. Typical bevels are around 30 degrees for plane irons, 35 degrees for chisels, and up to 40 degrees for marking knives. Ask an experienced saw filer to sharpen cutting tools that have more complex edge patterns (saws and drill bits, for example).

Grinding and honing are the usual methods for putting edges on your tools. Though there are many sharpening tools out there vying for your hard-earned dollars, the most useful are *wet grinders*, a selection of *water* and *oil whetstones*, and *wheeled honing guides*.

Sharpening a really dull edge begins with the grinding process and ends with honing. Grinding is best done on either a wet grinding wheel or a water-cooled belt grinder. The wet grinding wheel cools the tip of the tool with water as the tool is ground, ensuring that the steel's *temper* (degree of hardness) is not compromised by the friction-generated heat that typically occurs during dry grinding. A belt grinder, on the other hand, has the advantage of grinding a truly flat bevel; unlike a wheeled grinder, it won't leave a slightly concave surface on the tool edge. Any *wire edge* (a paper-thin sliver of metal that sometimes develops at the tip of the bevel during grinding) will be removed during honing.

Always adjust and tighten the tool rest of your grinder securely so that the tool's bevel corresponds to the surface of the grinding wheel or belt. A medium-grit grinding surface is effective for most jobs. Apply slight pressure to the tool as you grind it and remove only enough metal to reshape the edge cleanly.

Honing usually refers to the process of sharpening on either man-made or natural stones, which are available through catalogues and woodworking-supply stores. A useful set of stones might include an inexpensive, coarse, man-made oilstone and a more costly, finer-grit natural stone such as a novaculite stone. Water stones are also available; some people prefer them, particularly for final honing to razor sharpness. Select stones that are large enough to accommodate the edges of the tools you'll be sharpening.

Lubricate the stone with a generous amount of light penetrating oil or with water, depending upon the type of stone. This will help you achieve a rhythmic honing action, and the oil or water will preserve the stone's textured surface by floating the tiny bits of ground metal away from it. As you

work, wipe off the stone and replace the oil or water frequently.

Set the tool's bevel flat upon the stone, applying pressure on the tool's back; the bevel should remain parallel to the stone's surface at all times. Move the tool in either a figure-eight motion or in a back-and-forth manner. While you sharpen, float the bevel across the stone so that you're using all its parts. Turn the tool over occasionally and hone the flat side; examine both sides often to judge how you're doing. A shiny, dressed surface indicates that you're making progress. Duller spots should be surfaced with more honing. If a wire edge develops, continue honing to remove it.

An alternative method of honing is to fasten the tool in a wheeled honing guide. This handy tool adjusts for any bevel and is particularly useful for sharpening wide plane irons.

For an edge you can shave with, move on to a fine stone. Hone in a similar fashion, checking the edge now and then by carefully running a thumbnail along its toe. If it glides along the edge without catching on tiny rough spots, you're ready for work!

Clamping Tools

Many types of clamps are available, but only three are used to secure the parts of projects in this book: C-clamps, quick clamps, and spring clamps (also known as squeeze clamps). All clamps are limited in their usefulness by their throat depth and by the open distance between their jaws. Clamps can be purchased second-hand at great savings; just be certain that the various parts of any used clamp are in good working order and alignment before you buy.

Note that clamps are not included in the tools lists provided in the projects. They're considered a must for any woodworking venture.

C-CLAMP

This general purpose clamp is useful for securing small parts together. You'll need 6" clamps for building these projects; in some instances, as many as a dozen are used at one time. (The 6" figure represents the widest jaw distance with the clamp screw open.)

QUICK CLAMP

With one fixed jaw and another that slides along a narrow bar for instant adjustment, the quick clamp is ideal for rapidly securing multiple parts during glue-up. Available in a wide variety of lengths, these clamps are also useful for clamping longer parts together.

SPRING CLAMP

This overgrown clothespin is perfect for temporarily clamping parts together without glue so that you can check for correct alignment. Use the smallest sizes for clamping together featherweight balsawood parts.

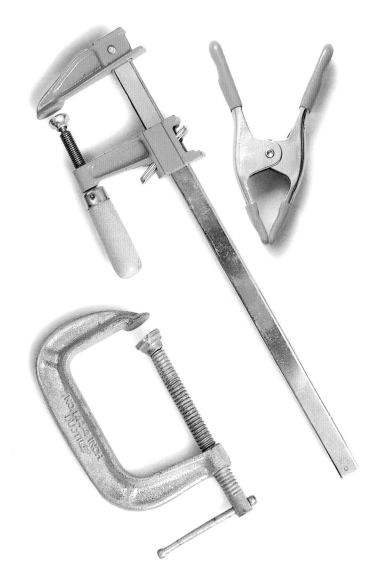

Hammers and Mallets

Of the many available tools for striking, just two are essential for building these projects: a claw hammer and a bench mallet. Add other hammers and mallets to your collection as you need them.

16-OUNCE CLAW HAMMER

This tool is used for nail driving, nail pulling, and miscellaneous banging and bumping tasks. Balance is critical with any hammer, so if you don't own one, test-drive a few at your dealer's before you buy.

BENCH MALLET

This traditionally patterned mallet is ideal for powering the chisels required for our projects. Its lightweight wooden construction packs a surprising wallop but is kinder to the wooden handles of tools such as chisels than a steel-headed hammer would be.

Screwdrivers

Installing a screw efficiently requires a screwdriver that is matched to the type and size of screw being used. For driving many screws quickly, purchase a *drive bit*; these are described on page 30.

PHILLIPS-HEAD SCREWDRIVER

For the No. 6 or No. 8 bugle-headed deck screws used extensively in this book, a No. 2 Phillips-head screwdriver will do the job nicely. The tip of this tool has an X-shaped tip to match the X-shaped slots in Phillips-head screws. Most types of screwdrivers are available in sizes No. 1 through No. 3, which have smaller and larger tips matched to smaller and larger screws, respectively. Screwdriver shafts also come in various lengths.

FLAT-BLADED SCREWDRIVER

This tool is designed for slotted screws and is sized similarly to the Phillips-head screwdriver.

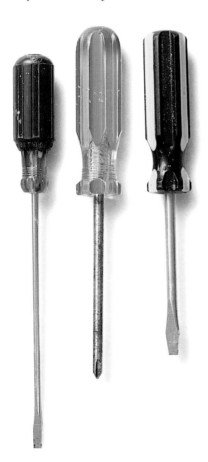

Miscellaneous Hand Tools

Listed below are four hand tools that will make shop work easier for you. These tools aren't included in the projects' tools lists, so make sure to have them on hand.

UTILITY KNIFE

You'll need this tool, along with a few replacement blades, for slicing and dicing.

BRAD SETTER

This finger-saver drives brads neatly with a simple push stroke, eliminating the fumbling involved with using a hammer. Purchase a high-quality brad setter for reliable performance.

NAIL SET

Used with a hammer, this tool sets nails just below the surface; the holes are then filled with wood filler.

AWL

Blunt-tipped drill bits such as twist-drill bits sometimes "skate" across wood when they're started into a boring layout. To prevent skating, use the sharp point of an awl to "dimple" the layout mark. Though the dimpling process isn't described in the project instructions, you should use it whenever skating might occur.

As you look through the project instructions, you'll notice that occasional references are made to common hand tools that aren't described in the previous pages or included in the projects' tools lists (adjustable wrenches, bastard-cut files, and hacksaws, for example). These are used for maintenance and for hardware applications. If you don't already own such tools, purchase them from your tool supplier, where information on their use is also available.

POWER TOOLS

Only five handheld power tools are necessary for building the projects in *Wood on Wheels*: the circular saw, jigsaw, variable-speed reversible drill, pad sander, and router. Although stationary power tools such as band saws, table saws, and drill presses do provide levels of accuracy and efficiency that are more difficult to achieve with portable power tools, space and budget limitations prevent many home shop owners from acquiring stationary equipment. The more complex operation of these power tools and the time and expense of their upkeep are also considerations. Unless your work involves complex patterns, precisely matched multiple parts, or commercial production schedules, you probably won't need the level of sophistication offered by these tools.

Handheld power tools have come a long way since they were first introduced. A visit to a well-stocked supplier will reveal some remarkably efficient workhorses with durable construction and precision electronic drives. While these tools can't perform all the operations that stationary tools can, they do have some real advantages. Their portability allows rapid setup anywhere you wish, including near a pair of sawhorses under a blue sky. Portable tools also accept a wide variety of standardized blades and bits that can be switched in a flash, offering you many different options as your work progresses.

Best of all, handheld power tools are easily mastered. Their setup and adjustment is straightforward, and their efficient operation allows your creativity to take charge. With a little time and patience, you'll soon be in complete control of the techniques required to build the projects this book.

Whenever you're building, be alert to the limitations of the tools you're using. The safe operation of power tools, in particular, is contingent on following the recommendations provided by their manufacturers and on your common sense and ability level. If you're a beginner, practice using your tools to execute basic techniques on well-secured scrap wood. Following are some additional safety tips:

- *Wear safety glasses whenever you're operating a power tool; hearing protectors are also recommended.*
- *Disconnect the power cord before making any tool adjustments.*
- *After making adjustments such as cutting depth and angle of cut, firmly tighten all tool parts before reconnecting the power cord.*
- *Always use clamps or a vise to secure your stock well.*
- *Keep a firm grip on your tool as you use it; never let your fingers out of your sight.*
- *Never force the action of any blade or bit; doing so is very dangerous, as is working with a blade or bit that is dull or damaged.*

Circular Saw

With a perpendicular cutting depth of 2-1/4" and a 45-degree cutting depth of 1-3/4", the circular saw is your primary power tool for stock preparation and straight saw cuts. The 7-1/4" circular saw, named for its blade diameter, is the standard size for general saw work.

Cutting across the stock's width and ripping along its length are a cinch with this saw. Attaching an optional rip fence to the saw will make ripping even easier; the fence can be adjusted for effortlessly exact cuts.

Two circular-saw blades are required for these projects: a carbide-tipped general-purpose blade for cutting solid stock and a plywood blade for cutting plywood. To change blades, select an adjustable or open-end wrench to fit the bolt that secures the saw's washer and blade. All saw blades remove a section of wood called a *kerf*, which is equal to the thickness of the teeth; don't forget to figure the kerf into your layouts and your purchase of materials.

Standard circular-saw cuts are made perpendicular to the stock's surface; angled cuts up to 45 degrees from the surface are made by adjusting the saw's body on its base and securing it with a thumbscrew. Angled cuts require particularly careful layouts, a steady guiding hand, and a sharp eye. When making any cut, be sure that the blade extends through the stock by 3/8" or the depth recommended by the manufacturer.

Jigsaw

In *Wood on Wheels*, this curve-cutting tool is used extensively to create the arcing shapes that add liveliness to the projects. The orbital blade action of high-quality jigsaws increases their cutting efficiency by moving the blade in an orbital motion, rather than in the up-and-down reciprocal motion of lesser-quality tools. Some jigsaws offer base adjustment similar to that of circular saws.

Jigsaw blades are made for different materials, including solid wood, plywood, and soft metals. *Medium-toothed general-purpose blades* cut solid stock smoothly and quickly. *Plywood blades* make exceptionally clean cuts in plywood stock. *Scrolling blades* are used for tight curves; they mimic the action of fretsaws. This last type of blade is adept at sawing radii too small for ordinary jigsaw blades. Triangularly-shaped blades known as *flush-cutting blades* are useful for sawing into corners or other projections. To avoid unnecessary trips to your supplier's, always keep extra blades handy.

Variable-Speed Reversible (VSR) Drill

A 3/8" chuck capacity is fine for most applications, although a 1/2" capacity is ideal. Use the key supplied with your drill to secure the bits in the chuck. Keyless drills, which tighten by twisting a collar around the chuck, are also available. Cordless drills with a rechargeable battery feature are most useful for hardware installation.

As in all power-tool use, drilling involves the entire body. Secure the work low enough so that you can look squarely down onto the drill as it does its work and plant your feet firmly and comfortably. A drill bit that's started squarely into stock rarely wanders from its intended destination.

Drill guides, which aid in the accurate boring of straight holes, are available in a variety of styles, but they aren't as critical to accurate drilling as your own work habits! Always secure your stock, maintain the correct body position, and start the hole properly.

Drill bits are patterned to achieve different results. In the list that follows are the bits favored for working on our projects:

BRADPOINT BITS

Use these for typical hole-boring tasks. Their pointed tips prevent them from skating away from layout marks, and the double flutes on their shanks remove wood waste from the holes.

TWIST-DRILL BITS

These medium-efficiency drill bits lack the bradpoint feature but are available in sizes much smaller than are bradpoint bits.

FORSTNER BITS

These remarkable bits bore clean, flat-bottomed holes and are available in larger sizes than are bradpoint bits. Expensive to purchase and tough to sharpen, Forstner bits are most useful for boring shallow holes where accuracy is critical.

COUNTERSINK BITS

These conical bits create hollows to match the size of screw heads, allowing screws to be countersunk flush with or below the stock's surface. Holes for the screw shafts must be bored separately.

PILOT BITS

These one-step drill bits bore a countersunk screw hole for the screw's entire length. Pilot bits are available for different screw sizes, and adjustable *stop collars* on them provide a measure of depth control. Whenever possible, project parts that will be fastened together with screws should be pilot-bored while clamped together as a unit; as a space-saving device, the project instructions in this book often omit this commonsense step.

PHILLIPS-HEAD DRIVE BITS

Chuck these work-savers into your drill whenever you have numerous screws to drive; they serve as power-driven screwdrivers. A No. 2 drive bit is most useful for the No. 6 and No. 8 deck screws used in our projects.

HOLE SAW

This ingenious gadget is necessary for making the small wheels of some projects and is an excellent investment for the motion-toy builder. Its mandrel is secured by a set screw to a guide bit that resembles a twist-drill bit. The actual sawing is done by the hole saw itself, which is a cup-shaped, toothed device screwed onto the mandrel. Available in different sizes, hole saws are best purchased as sets. For instructions on using them to create wheels, turn to "Round Trip" on pages 36 to 39.

Router

While the bits for this tool provide endless options for shaping any part of your stock, the routing in this book serves only to shape the *arrises* (or junctures between surfaces) of project parts. A 1/2"-capacity router often includes adjustable stops, which allow the builder to control the boring depth easily.

Routing is best accomplished in several passes; adjust the bit each time for a deeper cut. Whenever possible, rout long-grain *arrises* before routing adjacent cross-grain arrises; this will help prevent the stock from splintering at the corners. Two router bits are used in this book.

CHAMFER BIT

This is a 45-degree edging bit that can be adjusted to create *chamfers* (or bevels) of different widths.

3/8" AND 1/4" ROUNDING-OVER BITS

These bits shape rounded arrises that are 3/8" and 1/4" in size.

Pad Sander

Used to remove tool marks from project parts, the pad sander saves wear and tear on your arms by eliminating much of the hand-sanding necessary for getting your projects to the finish line. Pad sanders grip small pieces of sandpaper, which must be changed frequently for best results.

Orbital pad sanders are more effective than the older pad sanders that operate with a simple back-and-forth motion. Always run the sander in the same direction as the wood's grain, and keep the tool in constant motion while it's in contact with the surface of the wood.

For large surfaces, a *belt sander* will save you time because its rotating belt sands surfaces much more vigorously than a pad sander can. While belt sanders are extremely efficient, the relatively small surface areas of the project parts in *Wood on Wheels* do not dictate the need for this tool.

SANDPAPER

After a project is tooled to shape, sandpaper is the key to a smooth, ready-to-finish surface. Choose the right sandpaper for the job at hand. *Flint, garnet,* and *aluminum-oxide papers* are common choices; each is named for the type of crushed rock fragments glued to the paper backing. Flint paper, the least expensive, does a fair job but doesn't last very long. Garnet paper cuts quickly and is very durable. Aluminum-oxide paper is costly, but it doesn't fill with debris as fast as other papers and has a highly effective smoothing action.

If possible, purchase sandpaper sheets in quantity. *Grit sizes* (measures of average rock-particle sizes) range from 40-grit to 600-grit. 100-grit paper is fine for smoothing most tool marks from solid stock and plywood, while 220-grit paper will remove the finer scratches. After you hand-sand your project with a scrap of 220-grit paper and give it a good dusting, it will be ready for finishing.

Materials

Just as required tools are kept to an absolute minimum for the projects in this book, so are the types of materials. Materials for these playthings were carefully chosen to fulfill specific functions: to ensure the projects' strength and durability and to prevent little fingers from finding problem areas such as splintered edges and sharp, ill-fitting hardware. Use only first-quality materials; motion toys in particular require high-quality parts to produce a sturdy finished product. Carefully examine lumber, hardware, and other supplies and reject any materials that don't meet your high standards.

This section provides thumbnail descriptions of some basic materials and their building characteristics. For more detailed information, ask for advice from your supplier.

LUMBER

Wood is a naturally "play-friendly" material and is the main ingredient in cooking up a great riding or rolling toy. The woods used in these projects are derived from the two great classes of trees: fast-growing *softwoods* and slower-growing *hardwoods*. Each type has generally different characteristics. Lumber from softwoods is relatively lower in density than that derived from hardwoods and is generally more economical to purchase. Pine is the softwood lumber used for these projects, but spruce, fir, and cedar may also be suitable; ask for a recommendation at your dealer's.

Higher-density hardwoods are more costly to purchase, but they have an advantage over softwoods in their strength and resilience. Poplar is used for most of the hardwood project parts, largely because it's affordable and widely available. Oak, ash, and maple are other hardwoods that can be used to produce especially handsome heirloom-quality playthings.

It's easy to shape both pine and poplar with basic tools; the choice of one over the other is generally based on poplar's greater strength for supporting large axle assemblies and the like. Due to its finer grain, poplar also exhibits especially crisp details when tooled with a router. Some projects also call for specialty wood products such as birch dowels and lightweight balsa wood.

Parts of a Board

Four terms accurately describe the various parts of *dimension lumber* (the uniformly sized boards available at building-supply stores): *face*, *edge*, *end*, and *arris*. Understanding these terms is critical for keeping your project parts oriented correctly as you work on them. On most purchased stock, the faces, edges, and ends are situated at 90-degree angles to one another, and the long grain runs along the longest dimension.

FACES
These are the wide surfaces found on opposite sides of a board or, when the stock is square in cross-section, on all four sides.

EDGES
These are the narrower sides adjacent to the faces.

ENDS
Guess where these are! The *end grain* is wood grain that runs perpendicular to the long grain.

ARRISES
These are the junctures where wood surfaces meet. You may know them as corners, but arrises is the more exact term!

Joints and Details

You'll join together the wooden project parts in several different ways. Following is a list of the joints and detail cuts used in this book:

BUTT JOINT
This basic joint is formed by aligning two project parts at a 90-degree angle to one another.

FACE JOINT
Fastening together the faces of two parts creates this joint.

MITER (OR MITERED) JOINT
A *miter cut* is an angled cut made across the stock's thickness. A *miter joint* occurs when two parts are fitted together with at least one miter cut. *Beveled miters* are angled cuts made across the stock's thickness and width; picture frames, for example, often make use of beveled miter joints.

LAP JOINTS
Two project parts form a lap joint when they cross over one another and wood is removed from one or both parts to form a notch that helps secure the joint. To make a *half-lap* joint, half the thickness of each part is removed so that the resulting joint has the same thickness as a single part.

CHAMFER

This is a small bevel along an arris and is created with either a tilted circular-saw blade or, more commonly, a chamfer bit installed in a router. The chamfers used in this book are 45 degrees.

ROUND-OVER

This smoothly rounded detail is machined using a rounding-over bit chucked in a router.

Lumber Dimensions

These days, dimension lumber has shrunk from the stout sizes of yesteryear. A board is now a 2 x 4 or a 1 x 8 in name only; these measurements are known in the building trades as *nominal* measurements. The *actual* measurements of nominal 2 x 4s and 1 x 8s are approximately 1-1/2" x 3-1/2" and 3/4" x 7-1/4", respectively.

The chart that follows provides basic information on converting nominal lumber sizes to actual measurements, but minor variations dictate that you measure your stock carefully before you begin building and adjust the project dimensions as necessary. Lumber is the product of individual mill handlers and also shrinks and expands noticeably as the weather changes.

SOFTWOOD LUMBER SIZES

Nominal	Actual
1 x 2	3/4" x 1-1/2"
1 x 4	3/4" x 3-1/2"
1 x 6	3/4" x 5-1/2"
1 x 8	3/4" x 7-1/4"
1 x 10	3/4" x 9-1/4"
1 x 12	3/4" x 11-1/4"
2 x 2	1-1/2" x 1-1/2"
2 x 4	1-1/2" x 3-1/2"
2 x 6	1-1/2" x 5-1/2"
2 x 8	1-1/2" x 7-1/4"
2 x 10	1-1/2" x 9-1/4"
2 x 12	1-1/2" x 11-1/4"
4 x 4	3-1/2" x 3-1/2"
4 x 6	3-1/2" x 5-1/2"
6 x 6	5-1/2" x 5-1/2"
8 x 8	7-1/2" x 7-1/2"

Plywood is often slightly thinner than its nominal thickness, too, because it receives a final sanding at the mill. A nominal 1/2"-thick piece may actually measure 15/32" or less.

Hardwood dowel sizes are specified in the projects. When a "Cut List" calls for a 1" x 36" dowel, for example, cut a 1"-diameter dowel to 36" in length.

Balsa wood, a crafts material, is available in various shapes and sizes from your local craft shop.

Lumber Grades and Defects

Lumber grades—measures of the number and types of defects in lumber—typically run from common, a less expensive grade with many defects, to clear, a more expensive and sound material. No matter which grade you use, hand-select your own lumber whenever possible. Keep in mind that slight defects generally don't compromise the strength of your lumber choices, and small knots and the like have a beauty all their own. Common defects include the following:

KNOTS

These defects occur at the junctures of limbs and tree trunks. While small pin knots are acceptable, large or loose knots are not.

CHECKS AND SPLITS

Lumber with separations along the long grain or across the end grain can create serious problems for the woodworker; don't purchase checked or split boards.

WANE

When boards are cut from felled timber, those cut closest to the rounded exterior of the log have broadly rounded arrises known as wane. Better grades of lumber won't present you with this problem.

WARPAGE

To judge the degree of twisting or bending present in any board, site along the board's length, from end to end. The short lumber sections called for in these projects can often be cut from slightly warped stock.

MISCELLANEOUS DEFECTS

Stains, grade stamps, and minor insect damage can often be patched or painted over so that they aren't visible in your completed project.

Exterior-Grade Lumber

If you're building motion toys for extensive outdoor use, substitute naturally decay-resistant lumber or pressure-treated lumber for the materials suggested. Because certain exterior-grade materials contain chemical preservatives, however, obtain details from your dealer on handling and building with these products in a manner that is safe for you and your kids.

HARDWARE AND GLUES

The projects in this book emphasize hardware fasteners rather than glue because metal fasteners are generally more reliable in toys that will receive hard use. Look for tips on hardware installation in the project instructions.

The best way to acquaint yourself with the many types of hardware and glues available is to stroll through the aisles at your supplier's. Because an exact fit is all-important where hardware is concerned, double-check your selections for size and other critical features before you head for the sales counter. You'll reap significant savings by purchasing hardware in bulk rather than in tiny plastic packages, and you'll minimize shopping trips, too. The following list represents the most common types of hardware used in this book:

PHILLIPS-HEAD DECK SCREWS
These screws are treated to resist corrosion, and their galvanized finish adds an attractive luster to finished play projects. Their bugle-shaped heads and finely-threaded, narrow shafts make deck screws a pleasure to install. Ordinary plated flathead screws are an acceptable substitute, except where outdoor toys are concerned.

FINISHING NAILS
Because these headless nails can be countersunk below the wood's surface, they can be completely hidden by applying wood filler over them. Small 3d, 4d, and 6d finishing nails are most appropriate for these projects.

BRADS AND WIRE NAILS
These small fasteners, available in many sizes, are used for securing thin project parts together. Brads are headless; wire nails have tiny flat heads.

CUT WASHERS AND LOCKING WASHERS
Washers serve as spacers on hardware installations and are available in standard sizes. Cut washers are flat and for general use, while locking washers help keep nuts tightened securely on hardware assemblies.

THREADED ROD, CAP NUTS, AND HEX NUTS
These products are matched in various sizes for assembly. Use a hacksaw to cut threaded rod to exact lengths. Cap nuts cover the rods' protruding ends to provide an additional safety factor. Hex nuts are for general use wherever tightening is needed.

STEEL TUBING
Used in conjunction with threaded rod to create axle assemblies, this product is sold in standard sizes and lengths. Cut steel tubing to length with a hacksaw.

SCREW EYES
These ring-headed screws are available in many sizes. Install them with slip-joint pliers.

ALUMINUM TUBING
This product, available in many sizes at craft stores, is used to make axle spacers and the like.

RUBBER-TIRED WHEELS
Available with or without ball-bearing hubs, these wheels are commonly used for lawn and garden equipment, but they're ideal for rolling toys as well. For a complete description of wheels and axle-assembly methods, turn to "Round Trip" on pages 36 to 39.

CASTERS
Available in many shapes and sizes, these wheeled mechanisms are perfect for motion toys. The project instructions detail the exact types of casters you'll need.

NYLON CORD
Braided nylon cord is inexpensive, available in many sizes, and often comes in bright colors; it's purchased by the linear foot. To prevent the ends from fraying, lightly roast them with a kitchen match.

MISCELLANEOUS HARDWARE
In the project instructions, you'll find descriptions of springs, angle braces, finishing washers, and other hardware that is used only occasionally. Purchase these items at your hardware store or at shops specializing in specific types of hardware.

ALIPHATIC RESIN GLUE
Also called *woodworker's glue* or simply *yellow glue*, this is the standard choice for gluing project parts together. Fast-setting and strong, it's unfortunately susceptible to moisture.

EPOXY RESIN GLUE
This two-part glue is super-strong and comes in either quick-setting or slow-setting form. Use it for your most problematic gluing jobs.

CONSTRUCTION ADHESIVE
This strong glue comes in a tube and is applied with a caulking gun. You'll need this adhesive for toys that are used extensively outdoors.

FINISHES

Finishes for riding and rolling toys should be attractive in appearance, protective of the wood's surface, and child-safe in formulation. With these basics in mind, feel free to make creative choices when selecting finishes. Your building-materials supplier may offer a variety of materials to get you started, but a visit to a full-service paint-supply shop will really get your motor running. Paint stores offer expert advisors when you run into finishing problems, so don't be bashful when those problems arise.

The one mistake that many novice builders (and some long-time builders who should know better) make is to assume that a project is done when the finishing stage is reached. This sometimes results in a slapdash attempt at finishing the project without the measured, step-by-step approach that characterized building it. Establish a thorough approach to your finishing work; you'll be surprised by the difference in appearance of the finished product.

Thorough *prep work* (or wood-surface preparation) is essential. Fill dents and scratches with wood filler and sand the surfaces with progressively finer grit sizes until you're satisfied that they're smooth. Then examine the surfaces under strong light and sand again. (*Flat light*, or light that is directed across a sanded surface from a very low angle towards your eyes, is the most effective sanding tool you'll ever own.) Complete your prep work by using a tack rag to wipe away every speck of sanding dust.

The type of finish you use will dictate the tools necessary for its application. Many finishes, including the ones used on these projects, are brushed on. Others are applied with a rag. Child-safe finishes, which are non-toxic and lead-free, are now widely available and are marked as such on their labels. While oil- or alkyd-based finishes are very durable, it's best not to use them on kids' playthings. Water-based finishes offer easy cleanup with warm water. Avoid treated lumber and all finishes when you're making toys for very young children who are still teething and apt to nibble on everything!

Finishing is best done under conditions of low humidity, with even temperatures well above 50°F (10°C). Never let finishing products freeze and keep them tightly covered and clean. To avoid the "skin" that develops on the surfaces of stored finishes, place a piece of plastic food wrap on the surface of the finish to separate it from the canned air that causes this problem; then replace the lid on the can. Keep the working tips of brushes and other tools dry and protect them from damage.

Apply finishes in a clean, well-ventilated environment. Use plenty of drop cloths and arrange your finishing tools and materials ahead of time so that you won't have to hunt up a brush while you work. Review the manufacturer's instructions on any container of finishing material before you lift the lid and follow these instructions carefully.

Brush with the grain and avoid overloading your brush; heavily laden brushes increase drying time and produce a lumpy, unattractive appearance. Sand each coat lightly and wipe away the dust, allowing each coat to dry completely before proceeding. For a professional look, finish as many parts as possible before project assembly.

A list of useful finishing tools and materials follows:

WOOD FILLER
Commercial fillers vary, but most require over-filling the blemishes to compensate for shrinkage. Apply the filler with a flexible spackling knife, mounding it slightly above the wood's surface. When the filler is quite dry, sand it to match the surface of the wood. For information on sanding products, review page 30.

LATEX WOOD PRIMER
Also known as *undercoater*, primer seals the pores in wood and ensures adhesion of the paints that are applied on top. Primer also acts as a shock absorber of sorts, discouraging enamels from chipping. You'll find that one coat of primer and two coats of enamel are worth a dozen coats of enamel applied straight to bare wood.

LATEX ENAMEL PAINT
These paints are available in a variety of designer colors, but if you'd like to mix your own, experiment by

combining the primary colors (red, yellow, and blue) with a bit of white or black. Do ask your dealer whether or not the paints you're purchasing will produce "true" mixed colors. Some reds and blues, for example, produce brown rather than purple when they're combined. Avoid mixing paints of different types or from different manufacturers. Enamel paints are available in matte, semigloss, and gloss finishes, which produce finished surfaces having no shine, a bit of luster, and a mirrorlike shine, respectively.

WATER-BASED CLEAR VARNISH
This tough, transparent finish is perfect for highlighting a project's wooden parts. Your dealer can provide a range of finishes from matte to gloss.

ARTIST'S ACRYLIC COLORS
Thin these tube paints with water and apply them with brushes to give the wood surface a dyed appearance and to provide effects not available with enamel paints. Purchase acrylics, which come in many colors, from art-supply stores. Avoid acrylics if your kids are still teething!

BRUSHES
Use synthetic-bristle brushes for water-based finishes. Though you'll want to select brushes to suit your particular needs, a few brushes are indispensable: 1/2", 1", and 2" flat brushes for painting large surfaces; and a liner brush for detail work. If you can afford them, *sash brushes*, which have angled tips to facilitate work in tight corners, are good additions to your brush collection. Shaped-tip brushes called *rounds* are available in graduated sizes and offer even more options for the serious finisher.

TACK RAGS, CLOTH RAGS, AND PAINT CUPS
Commercial tack rags will remove the finest sanding dust from your completed projects, while cloth rags are handy at cleanup time. To maintain your finishes in top condition and to keep them clean, avoid dipping your brushes directly into store-bought cans. Instead, use paint cups fashioned from cleaned cans and jars.

Round Trip

As the song says, "The wheels on the bus go round and round." And round is what makes a wheel a wheel! To keep your projects' wheels from going bump-bada-bump instead, read this section carefully. You'll have a smoother ride if you do.

WHEEL BASICS
Although ready-made wheels are widely available and can shorten assembly time, many of the projects in this book call for shop-built wheels. Why? Because the latter are less expensive and because they won't mar a handmade toy's appearance as store-bought wheels might.

The sizes of wheel-assembly parts and the types of wheel design vary from project to project. Three basic wooden wheel types (A, B, and C) are used in many of these projects. When uncommon wheel types are called for, specific instructions for making and/or assembling them are provided in the projects themselves. In order to avoid reinventing the wheel each time you start a new project, familiarize yourself with the basic instructions that follow.

Clear, warp-free materials are essential for making high-quality wheels; hardwoods are your best choice. While most axles in these projects are wooden, a few are metal. Specific instructions for assembling metal axles are given in the instructions for the projects that use them.

To make some wheels, you'll need a hole saw; see page 30 for a complete description of this tool. The largest one, for 3/4" wheels, is 1-3/8" in diameter. While a drill press used in conjunction with a hole saw ensures safe, accurate cutting of large-diameter wheels, the smaller-sized hole saws can be used in a handheld power drill if you secure the stock well and hold the drill in a 90-degree vertical position. Other essential tools include a jigsaw, a center finder, a compass, a hacksaw, and an adjustable wrench.

Successful wheels are carefully fabricated. Wheels that are out-of-round will give your project an unintended wobble, and axle holes bored at even a slight angle will create obvious problems when the axles are installed in them. Your goal is to make round wheels with "square" holes, but it's best to cut one or two extra wheels so that an occasional goof won't mean that you have to start from scratch.

The wheel sizes, materials, and designs for the projects in *Wood on Wheels* were chosen to support the size and weight of the projects. While 1/4" hardwood dowel axles and 1" wheels suit the smallest push and pull toys, beefy 1/2" steel-axle assemblies and large wheels are a must for older children's riding toys. Wherever possible, wheels are separated from adjacent wooden parts by means of washers or similar hardware. When designing playthings, always over-build for strength and make sure that all hardware will stay assembled for the life of the project.

Also bear in mind that the various wheel-and-axle combinations may be interchanged for different effects. Bob's Sled and the Puzzle Truck, for example, can be made to bob or wobble by making adjustments in their wheel designs. The following techniques offer some options.

Type A Rolling Wheels

These are simple, rolling wheels, which are fixed in position on their axles. For wheels smaller than 1-3/8" in diameter, use a hole saw to cut the wheel from stock. The 1/4" guide bit that fits smaller hole saws bores a centered 1/4" axle hole as it cuts the wheel. For larger axles on these small wheels, just use a larger hole-saw guide bit or enlarge the hole with a twist-drill bit. (Bradpoint bits and other sharp-tipped bits won't work.) Always hold the drill at a 90-degree angle to the stock's surface.

For wheels larger than 1-3/8", use a compass to scribe circles on the stock and then cut out the circles with a jigsaw and scrolling blade. To make sure the wheels are true, check their diameters with a tape measure and rasp or sand any high spots. Then locate the wheel centers with a center finder. Dimple the center mark and bore the axle hole with a bit that matches the diameter of the required axle.

You'll note that the wheels in some projects (the Space Cruiser and Trundle Block Wagon, for example), though they have centered through-holes, are not labeled as Type A wheels. These wheels are not fixed to their axles but instead rotate freely on them.

Type B Bobbing Wheels

Type B and Type A wheels differ in only one respect; in Type B wheels, the axle is offset from the center of the wheel to create a bobbing or hopping motion as the project rolls along.

Rather than cutting these wheels as Type A wheels and then plugging the centered hole left by the guide bit, use the "scoring" technique instead. First, adjust the guide bit so that it projects 3/16" below the hole saw's teeth and begin the wheel cut; stop the cut when the hole-saw teeth have penetrated to a depth of about 1/8". Then adjust the guide bit so that its tip is 7/8" behind the teeth, hidden within the hole saw's interior. Set the teeth on the scored stock and finish the cut. (Use this technique on small wheels only and never permit children to execute it!)

Flip the wheel over, locate its center, and measure the offset from that center. Finally, use a bit of the appropriate size to bore the offset axle hole. Install pairs of wheels so that the offset on each is positioned identically. (The Rollerboy project is an exception; it has only one Type B wheel.)

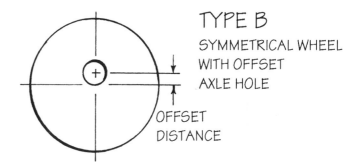

TYPE B
SYMMETRICAL WHEEL WITH OFFSET AXLE HOLE

OFFSET DISTANCE

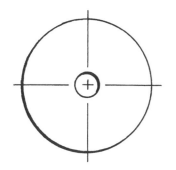

TYPE A
SYMMETRICAL WHEEL WITH CENTERED AXLE HOLE

Type C Wobbling Wheels

These wheels are made in the same way as Type B wheels, but they create an amusing crawling or swimming motion because they're installed so that the offsets on each pair of wheels are positioned 180 degrees from one another.

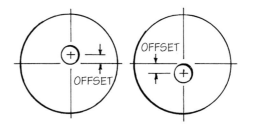

TYPE C
SYMMETRICAL WHEELS
WITH OPPOSING OFFSET
AXLE HOLES

AXLE TYPES

AXLE SUPPORTS

Simple Axle. The simplest of axle-installation methods is to bore holes in the project's sides or base—holes that are slightly larger than the diameter of the axles—and then use the holes as axle housings. Not all projects, however, can accommodate this method.

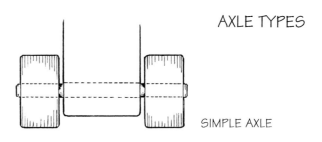

SIMPLE AXLE

Screw Eye Axle Support. One alternative is to use the "eye" portions of screw eyes as axle housings. When the wheels are located beneath the project's base, the screw eyes must be long enough to allow a 1/8" clearance between the top of the wheel and the bottom of the base.

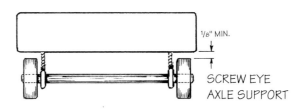

1/8" MIN.

SCREW EYE
AXLE SUPPORT

Wooden Axle Support. Another alternative is the use of axle supports. These pieces are cut from 3/4" or larger stock and are bored through their lengths with a bit slightly larger in diameter than the axle. (Straight boring is essential here!) The supports are fastened to the base with piloted deck screws driven either from the top face of the base or from the support's bottom face; the screws are located to avoid the axle.

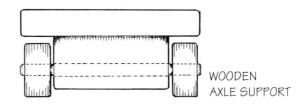

WOODEN
AXLE SUPPORT

Individual Axles. When axles can't be installed across the full width of a project, individual axles are located at each wheel location. In this setup, the wheels spin freely around fixed axles. The axle location is marked and dimpled and an axle-support hole at least 3/8" deep is bored to match the thickness of the axle. After the axle is glued into place, a centered pilot hole is bored through the opposite side of the hole and a screw is inserted to permanently fasten the axle in place.

Axles in this type of assembly must be long enough to accommodate both the wheel and a pin that is used to keep the wheel from slipping off the free end of the axle. This dowel pin is about one-third the diameter of the axle; it's inserted with a bit of glue into a hole of the same diameter bored through the axle's thickness just beyond the wheel's outside face.

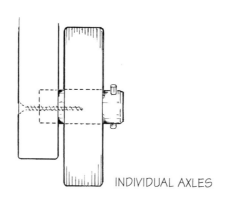

INDIVIDUAL AXLES

SECURING WHEEL-AND-AXLE ASSEMBLIES

Wooden wheels shrink and expand. While glue may secure them to their axles temporarily, a more reliable method is to secure them with a finishing nail or brad driven through the edge of the wheel circumference and into the axle. Align the wheel and axle exactly and mark the center of the curved wheel edge. Then use a pilot bit slightly longer than the wheel's radius to bore a hole through the wheel to accommodate a finishing nail or brad of an appropriate size. The bit should pierce the axle. Tap the fastener gently into this hole.

STEEL WHEELS AND AXLES

The rubber-tired steel-hubbed wheels used in *Wood on Wheels* have integral ball bearings that allow the wheels to rotate freely around the hubs. For safety's sake, purchase quality wheels that have a load capacity equal to their intended use.

The following suggestions use the Garden Cart project as an example. In this arrangement, a 1/2" O.D. (or outside diameter) steel tube, supported by a pair of wooden axle supports, passes through the wheels' hubs. A length of 3/8" threaded rod runs through the tube and extends beyond its ends. The rod is secured by lock washers and cap nuts, which tighten against the ends of the tube.

Because wheel dimensions vary, successful installation depends upon specific measurements. See the Garden Cart example that follows:

Hub length (the axle bore end-to-end) = 1-3/8"

Hub bore (the bore's I.D. or inside diameter) = 1/2"

Wheel size (the wheel's diameter and thickness) = 8" x 1-3/4"

The Garden Cart's hub length is less than its tread width. To provide clearance between the rubber wheel's edge and the side of the cart, several 1/2" cut washers are used as spacers between the wooden axle supports and the wheel hubs.

To determine the correct tube length for an assembly of this type, use this simple formula:

Length between the axle supports' outside faces

+ Hub length x 2

+ Space between hubs and supports required to provide clearance between the tires and the projects' sides

+ 1/4"

After assembly, each hub should have 1/8" "wiggle room" on the axle tube. To determine threaded rod length, add 1/2" to the tubing's length. Coupled with exact tire measurements, the use of smaller or larger hardware will allow any number of creative wheel-and-axle applications.

LUBRICATION

For a smoother rolling action with wooden axles and wheels, wax the parts occasionally with a candle stub. Lightweight lubricating oil will keep metal wheel-and-axle combinations spinning freely.

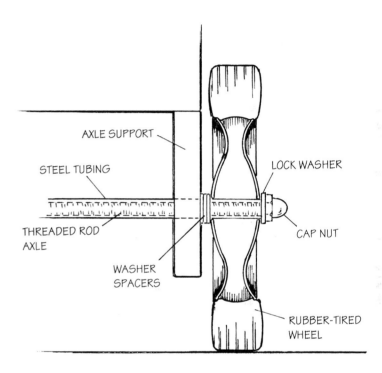

● ● ● ●

While it does require some effort to bring a measure of order and efficiency to your use of tools, techniques, and materials, you'll find that building the motion toys in this book is a real pleasure. Keep a firm grip on your tools and a steady eye on your goals and in no time at all, you'll be sharing some very special toys with your kids!

the PROKECTS

the PROJECTS
• • • •

Now for the fun! While the particulars of tools, techniques, and materials are important, building the projects is what Wood on Wheels *is really all about. Your kids will enjoy selecting projects and helping to build them as much as you do.*

The motion toys and related projects that are featured in this section are grouped in three categories: *"Small Wonders," "Rock and Roll," and "Movin' On." Each category offers toys that are broadly related as push and pull toys, larger riding and rolling toys, and specialty toys.*

As you examine the projects, note that each one includes a complete "Cut List," "Hardware and Supplies" list, and a list of "Suggested Tools." In many projects, you'll also find a special "Tips" section. The step-by-step instructions will guide you as you build. Skim the tips, the various lists, and the project instructions before you begin; doing so will ensure that you have the necessary tools and materials on board.
Now, get moving!

RAMBLIN' RABBIT

●●●●

This four-wheeled bunny has a pair of carrots for the road and articulated parts that your kids can position themselves.

CUT LIST

1 Torso • 3/4" x 4-1/2" x 9-3/4"
2 Legs • 3/4" x 4-3/4" x 6"
2 Arms • 3/4" x 1-1/2" x 4-3/8"
2 Ears • 3/4" x 1-7/8" x 6-7/8"
1 Base • 3/4" x 5-1/2" x 11"
4 Wheels (Type A) • 3/4" x 3-1/4"-diameter
2 Axles • 3/8" x 7-5/8" dowel
2 Carrots • 3/4" x 1" x 3-5/8"
2 Carrot dowels • 1/4" x 1" dowel

HARDWARE AND SUPPLIES

4 1-1/2" deck screws
6 No. 8 x 1-1/4" oval-head wood screws
4 6d finishing nails
1 Size 112 small screw eye
4 Size 12 screw eyes
6 Size 10 finishing washers
1 36" length of decorative cord

SUGGESTED TOOLS

Layout tools
Backsaw and miter box
Circular saw
Jigsaw with medium-toothed blade
Rasps
Claw hammer
No. 2 Phillips screwdriver
3/8" drill
1/4" and 3/8" bradpoint bits
1/16", 1/8", and 9/32" twist-drill bits
Pilot bit for 1-1/2" deck screws
Pad sander

TIP

• *Oval-head screws, which fit neatly with the finishing washers on this project, are commonly available at hardware suppliers. Because weather-related moisture will shrink and swell the project's parts, you may need to tighten or loosen these screws now and then to keep the parts easily adjustable.*

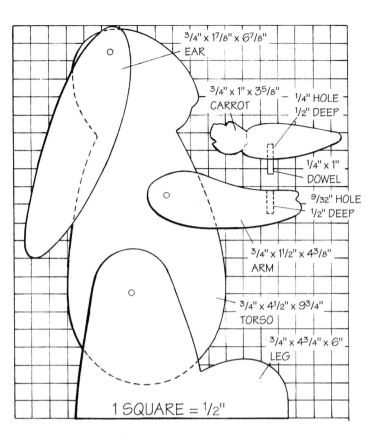

3/4" x 1⁷/₈" x 6⁷/₈"
EAR

3/4" x 1" x 3⁵/₈"   ¼" HOLE
CARROT   ½" DEEP

¼" x 1"
DOWEL

9/32" HOLE
½" DEEP

3/4" x 1½" x 4³/₈"
ARM

3/4" x 4½" x 9³/₄"
TORSO

3/4" x 4³/₄" x 6"
LEG

1 SQUARE = ½"

RAMBLIN' RABBIT

INSTRUCTIONS

1. Enlarge the five cutting patterns for the ears, torso, legs, arms, and carrots, and transfer them to 3/4" stock. Except for the single torso pattern, all others should be cut twice, for a total of nine pieces.

2. Mark the ten hole placements on the ears, arms, legs, and carrots: six holes for oval-head screws with finishing washers (through the arms, legs, and ears); a hole in the upper edge of each arm; and a hole in the lower edge of each carrot.

3. Cut out the pieces with your jigsaw and medium-toothed blade.

4. With a 1/8" twist-drill bit, bore a through-hole at each of the marks on the faces of the ears, arms, and legs.

5. Clamp the arms, top edges up, securely to your work surface. With a 9/32" twist-drill bit flagged for a 1/2" depth, bore the marked holes in their top edges.

6. Secure the carrots to your work surface, bottom edges up and, using a 1/4" bradpoint bit, bore 1/2"-deep holes at the marked locations.

7. With a backsaw and miter box, cut the two 1/4" x 1" carrot dowels. Also mark and cut two 7-5/8" lengths of 3/8" dowel to serve as axles.

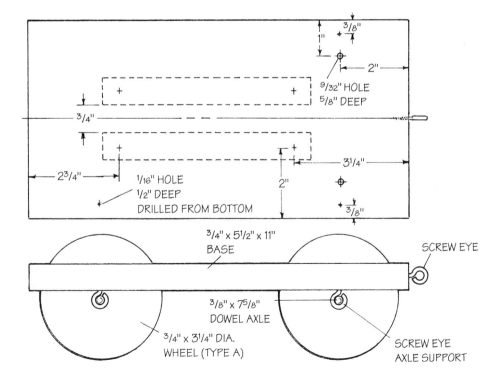

3/8"
1"
2"
9/32" HOLE
5/8" DEEP

3/4"

1/16" HOLE
½" DEEP
DRILLED FROM BOTTOM

2³/₄"

3¼"

2"

3/8"

3/4" x 5½" x 11"
BASE

SCREW EYE

3/8" x 7⁵/₈"
DOWEL AXLE

3/4" x 3¼" DIA.
WHEEL (TYPE A)

SCREW EYE
AXLE SUPPORT

8. Lay out the base and cut it to size with your circular saw. On its top face, mark the two 9/32" hole locations for the carrot dowels.

9. Bore these two holes, each 5/8" deep, using a 9/32" bit.

10. Flip the base over and, using a 1/8" bit flagged for a 1/2" depth, bore four pilot holes for the screw eyes that will accept the wheel axles. Each hole is located 3/8" from an edge and 2" from an end.

11. With a 1/16" bit, bore a hole into the center of the front end of the base.

12. With your pilot bit, bore the four holes in the bottom of the base for the deck screws that will fasten the legs in place. One pair of holes is located 2-3/4" from the rear end of the base and 2" from each edge. The other pair is located 3-1/4" from the front end and 2" from each edge.

13. Lay out four 3/4" x 3-1/4"-diameter Type A wheels and cut them out with your jigsaw (see page 37). With a 3/8" bradpoint bit, bore an axle hole through the center of each wheel. Take your time and you'll produce wheels that go round and round, rather than up and down!

14. Use your rasps and sandpaper to remove all tool marks from every part, smoothing each one carefully. Pay particular attention to smoothing arrises so that little fingers won't find any splinters later on. Round the ends of the 3/8" dowel axles carefully.

15. Finish the parts with at least two coats of any durable finish. Our Ramblin' Rabbit was finished with two coats of water-based satin varnish. Its face was detailed with gloss black enamel paint. The carrots were painted with orange and green acrylic paints, which provide a handsome semitransparent finish similar to a stain; for added protection, they were also given a coat of water-based satin varnish.

16. Set the two legs over the pilot holes in the base so that their inner faces are 3/4" apart. Check to see that they run parallel to the length of the base and secure them in place by driving 1-1/2" deck screws through the pilot holes.

17. Position the torso between the legs, with the figure's face pointing towards the carrot-dowel holes in the base.

18. To secure each leg to the torso, slip an oval-head screw through a finishing washer and drive the screw through the 1/8" hole in the leg. In the unlikely event that the two screws strike one another, remove the second screw and bore another through-hole in that leg, locating the second hole at a slight distance from the original one.

19. Attach the arms and ears in a similar fashion. Remember that the 9/32" holes in the edges of the arms should face up.

20. Use a drop or two of glue to secure the carrot dowels in the holes in the carrots.

21. Insert the four screw eyes into the four 1/8" holes in the bottom face of the base, turning their open eyes parallel to the edges of the base.

22. Slide the axles through the pairs of screw eyes and place pairs of wheels on the axles' ends. If the dowels don't slide easily through the eyes, open each eye slightly with a pair of slip-joint pliers.

23. Position each wheel so that its inside face is 1/16" from the edge of the base. Check to see that the dowels extend an equal distance beyond the wheels' outside faces.

24. Secure each wheel to its axle with a 6d finishing nail (see page 39).

25. Install a small screw eye in the hole in the end of the base. Attach a 36" length of decorative cord to the screw eye and you're done!

ROLLERBOY

• • • •

This bouncing three-wheeler captures the happy spirit of a child on the go.

CUT LIST

- 1 Body • 3/4" x 3-7/8" x 6"
- 2 Legs • 3/4" x 2-9/16" x 3-3/8"
- 2 Arms • 3/4" x 1-1/8" x 2-1/2"
- 2 Front wheels (Type A) • 3/4" x 1-3/8"-diameter
- 1 Rear wheel (Type B) • 5/8" x 2-1/4"-diameter
- 1 Front axle • 1/4" x 4-1/8" dowel
- 1 Rear axle • 1/4" x 1-1/4" dowel

HARDWARE AND SUPPLIES

- 2 No. 18 x 3/4" brads
- 8 3d finishing nails
- 1 4d finishing nail
- 4 1/4" cut washers

SUGGESTED TOOLS

Layout tools
Backsaw and miter box
Circular saw
Jigsaw with scrolling blade
Rasps
Claw hammer
3/8" drill
9/32" bradpoint bit
1/32" and 3/32" twist-drill bits
1-3/8" hole saw with 1/4" guide bit
Pad sander

INSTRUCTIONS

1. Enlarge the arm, leg, and body patterns to the sizes indicated and transfer them onto 3/4" stock. Mark locations for the 3d finishing nails and the 9/32" axle holes in the arms and legs. (Note that the 9/32" holes in the rear legs will be bored in the inside faces only.)

2. Cut out the three pieces, using your jigsaw and scrolling blade.

3. With your drill and a 1-3/8" hole saw with 1/4" guide bit, cut the two Type A front wheels from 3/4" stock (see page 37).

4. Using your compass, lay out the 2-1/4"-diameter Type B wheel on 3/4" stock and cut it out with your jigsaw.

5. To reduce the rear wheel's thickness to 5/8", use your flat rasp and 60- or 80-grit sandpaper to remove 1/8" of wood from one face. Be sure that the wheel is of even thickness.

6. With your center finder, locate the center of the rear wheel and mark it. Lay out a radius line from the

TIPS

- *Steps 4 and 5 describe how to make the 5/8"-thick rear wheel from a scrap of 3/4"-thick stock.*

- *With a bit of creativity, you can change your Rollerboy into a Rollergirl for a favorite daughter or granddaughter.*

center to the circumference of the circle. Mark a point on the line, 5/32" from the wheel's center, and bore a 1/4" through-hole at that point. (This eccentric hole placement creates the completed project's bobbing motion as it rolls along.)

7. Bore the 9/32" axle through-holes in the arms. Then bore the 9/32" holes for the rear wheel, 3/8" deep, on the inside faces of the legs. Finally, bore the marked 3/32" through-holes at the finish-nail locations in each arm and the leg.

8. Mark and cut the front and rear axles from 1/4" dowel stock.

9. Sand all parts carefully; if you wish, break the arrises with a rasp before sanding. The ends of the front axle should be carefully rounded.

10. Position the rear axle in the rear wheel so that an equal length of axle protrudes from each face. Then bore a 3/32" hole, 1-1/4" deep, into the edge of the wheel so that the drill bit pierces the axle. Secure the wheel in place by driving a 4d finishing nail into the hole.

11. Place a few drops of glue on the inside faces of the legs, taking care not to get any on the lower portions (the shins and feet). Slip a washer onto each end of the axle, place the axle's ends into the rear legs' 3/8"-deep holes, and position the legs around the rear of the body. Clamp the legs in place and make sure that the wheel spins freely in the cutout on the bottom of the body; if it doesn't, adjust the legs as necessary.

12. When the assembly has dried, remove the clamp and further secure the legs by gently driving 3d finishing nails into the 3/32" holes.

13. Secure the two arms with glue and 3d finishing nails, aligning the axle holes before driving the nails.

14. Slide the front axle through the holes in the front legs and slip a washer onto each end. Place the front wheels over the washers, positioning them so they turn freely but are as close to the washers as possible. An equal length of axle should protrude from each wheel's outside face. Secure the wheels with brads (see page 39).

15. After priming all parts, paint your Rollerboy in any way you wish, using bright, contrasting colors of latex enamel paints.

ROLLERBOY

1 SQUARE = 1/2"

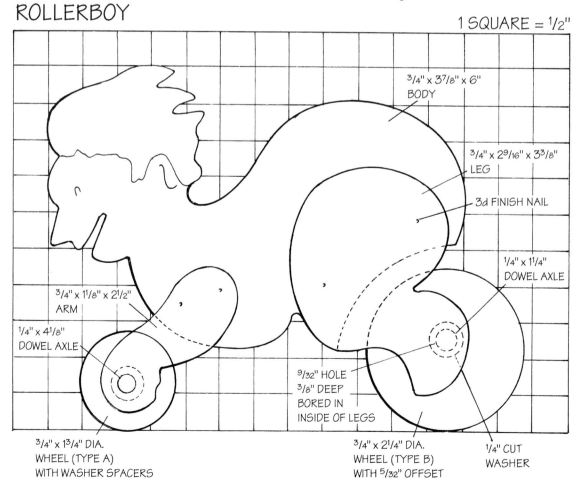

3/4" x 3⁷/₈" x 6"
BODY

3/4" x 2⁹/₁₆" x 3³/₈"
LEG

3d FINISH NAIL

1/4" x 1¹/₄"
DOWEL AXLE

9/32" HOLE
3/8" DEEP
BORED IN
INSIDE OF LEGS

3/4" x 1¹/₈" x 2¹/₂"
ARM

1/4" x 4¹/₈"
DOWEL AXLE

3/4" x 1³/₄" DIA.
WHEEL (TYPE A)
WITH WASHER SPACERS

3/4" x 2¹/₄" DIA.
WHEEL (TYPE B)
WITH ⁵/₃₂" OFFSET

1/4" CUT
WASHER

FRED FLOUNDER

• • • •

*Fred's swimming motion, caused by
eccentrically bored wheels, will really tickle your kids.*

CUT LIST

1 Figure • 3/4" x 6-7/8" x 12"
2 Axles • 1/4" x 4-3/4" dowel
2 Axle supports • 3/4" x 1-1/4" x 2-7/8"
4 Wheels (Type C) • 3/4" x 1-3/8"-diameter

HARDWARE AND SUPPLIES

4 1-1/4" deck screws
4 No. 18 x 3/4" brads
1 Size 112 small screw eye
1 36" length of decorative cord
  Wood filler

SUGGESTED TOOLS

Layout tools
Backsaw and miter box
Circular saw
Jigsaw with medium-toothed blade
Rasps
Claw hammer
No. 2 Phillips screwdriver
3/8" drill
1/16", 1/4", and 9/32" twist-drill bits
Pilot bit for 1-1/4" deck screws
1-3/8" hole saw with 1/4" guide bit
Router with 3/8" rounding-over bit
Pad sander
Spackling knife

INSTRUCTIONS

1. Enlarge the pattern of Fred's figure and transfer it, as well as the deck-screw pilot-hole locations, to 3/4" stock.

2. Cut out the shape with your jigsaw and medium-toothed blade.

3. Secure the figure to your work surface and use your router to round all the arrises on its top face, except those on the tail notch. Repeat to round the arrises on the bottom face.

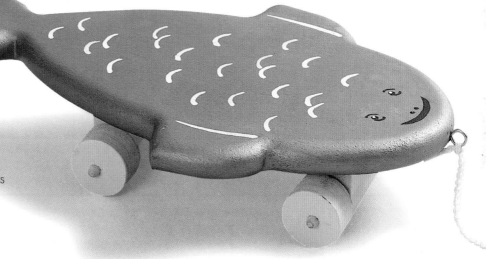

TIPS

• *To heighten the "floating" illusion of this pull toy, finish the wheels, axles, and axle supports in a natural-looking satin varnish that contrasts with the painted fish figure.*

• *Use extra caution when you operate a circular saw to cut small parts such as the axle supports.*

4. Bore pilot holes for 1-1/4" deck screws at the four marked locations on the upper face of the figure, counterboring each hole slightly so that the screw heads will sit just below the surface of the wood.

5. Lay out the two axle supports and cut them to length with your circular saw.

6. Bore a 9/32" hole through each axle support, from end to end. Locate each hole 7/8" from either 3/4" edge of the axle support and center it between the support's 1-1/4" faces.

7. Use your drill and 1-3/8" hole saw with 1/4" guide bit to cut out four 3/4" x 1-3/8"-diameter Type C wheels (see the detail of the wheels and page 38).

8. Position the figure with its counterbored surface face down. Locate the 3/4" edge of an axle support that is farthest from the 9/32" through-hole; then set that edge over one pair of pilot holes in the figure. Adjust the support so that its length is centered across the figure's width and runs perpendicular to the figure's length.

9. Holding the pieces in position, carefully clamp them together. Turn the figure face up and insert two deck screws through the figure and into the support.

10. Repeat Steps 8 and 9 to attach the second axle support so that its inner edge is 4-5/8" from the inner edge of the first support. (Use a straightedge to ensure that the ends of the supports are parallel to one another.)

11. Fill the counterbores with wood filler and let the filler dry thoroughly.

12. With a 1/16" twist-drill bit flagged for a 3/4" boring depth, bore a hole into the figure's chin.

13. Using your backsaw and miter box, cut the two 1/4" x 4-3/4" axles to length.

14. Rasp and sand all parts thoroughly.

15. Assemble the wheels and axles in the axle supports, positioning each wheel with its inner face 1/16" from the end of the support; each end of an axle should protrude an equal distance from each wheel.

16. Use brads to secure the wheels to the axles (see page 39).

17. Prime the figure with latex primer; leave the axle supports unfinished. After cleaning your brush, put at least two coats of water-based satin varnish on the axle supports and other remaining parts, sanding lightly and removing the dust between coats.

18. When the primer is dry, finish the figure with two coats of silver latex enamel; let each coat dry well. Then detail the figure with white and black latex enamel paint. The toy shown in the photo boasts scales, eyes, a "nose," and a goofy grin.

19. Fasten the screw eye into the pilot hole in the figure's chin, attach the decorative cord to it, and let your kids take Fred for a swim!

FRED FLOUNDER

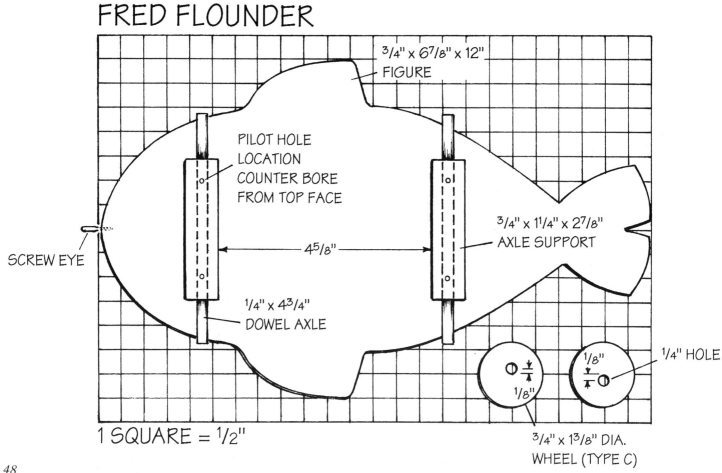

3/4" x 6⅞" x 12" FIGURE

PILOT HOLE LOCATION COUNTER BORE FROM TOP FACE

3/4" x 1¼" x 2⅞" AXLE SUPPORT

4⅝"

SCREW EYE

1/4" x 4¾" DOWEL AXLE

1/8"

1/8"

1/4" HOLE

1 SQUARE = ½"

3/4" x 1⅜" DIA. WHEEL (TYPE C)

HUNGRY GATOR

● ● ● ●

Watch out! This pearly toothed predator's wobble-action jaws really mean business.

CUT LIST

1 Body • 3/4" x 3-1/2" x 19-1/8"
2 Front legs • 3/4" x 1-1/8" x 4-1/8"
2 Rear legs • 3/4" x 2-5/8" x 2-5/8"
2 Jaws • 1/4" x 7/8" x 3-3/16"
1 Counterbalance • 1/4" x 15/16" x 5-7/8"
1 Log • 1/4" x 3-1/2" x 12-3/4"
1 Pond • 1/4" x 5-1/2" x 15-1/2"
1 Small lily pad • 1/4" x 7/8"-diameter
2 Large lily pads • 1/4" x 1-1/4"-diameter
2 Axle supports • 3/4" x 1-1/4" x 2-1/2"
2 Axles • 1/4" x 4-3/8" dowel
4 Wheels (Type A) • 3/4" x 1-1/4"-diameter

HARDWARE AND SUPPLIES

8 1" deck screws
3 No. 18 x 1/2" brads
4 No. 18 x 5/8" brads
1 3d finishing nail
1 Size 112 small screw eye
1 1/4" x 1-3/4" threaded rod, carriage bolt, or hex-head bolt
1 36" length of decorative cord
Quick-setting epoxy resin glue

SUGGESTED TOOLS

Layout tools
Backsaw and miter box
Circular saw
Coping saw or fretsaw
Jigsaw with scrolling blade
1/4" paring or firmer chisel
Rasps
Claw hammer
No. 2 Phillips screwdriver
3/8" drill
1/4" bradpoint bit
1/32", 1/16", and 9/32" twist-drill bits
Pilot bit for 1" deck screws
1-1/4" hole saw with 1/4" guide bit
Pad sander
Wire-cutting pliers

TIPS

- *You'll find small tubes of artist's acrylic colors at an art-supply store.*
- *Use extra care when sawing small parts with your circular saw.*
- *To take the "ache" out of prep work on highly detailed projects, sit in a comfortable chair and make sure that you have appropriate lighting.*

INSTRUCTIONS

1. Enlarge the cutting patterns for the body, legs, jaws, counterbalance, pond, log, and lily pads. Then carefully transfer them to the required stock (see "Cut List"). Note that these patterns also serve as placement guides. Be sure to transfer the boring patterns, too, including those for the eyes and nostrils.

2. Cut the parts to size, using a jigsaw and scrolling blade. Make the detail cuts on the smallest parts before the release cuts that free these pieces from the stock. You may find a coping saw or fretsaw useful for the most delicate cuts.

3. Lay out the two axle supports and cut them to size with your circular saw.

4. With your backsaw and miter box, cut the two axles to 4-3/8" in length.

HUNGRY GATOR

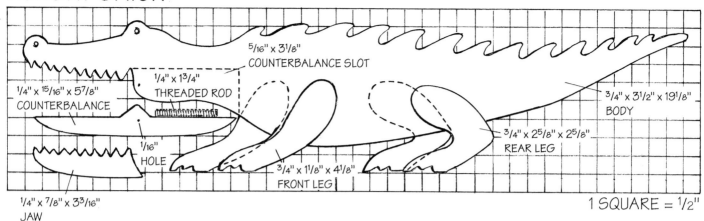

5/16" x 3 1/8"
COUNTERBALANCE SLOT

1/4" x 1 3/4"
THREADED ROD

1/4" x 15/16" x 5 7/8"
COUNTERBALANCE

1/16"
HOLE

3/4" x 3 1/2" x 19 1/8"
BODY

3/4" x 2 5/8" x 2 5/8"
REAR LEG

3/4" x 1 1/8" x 4 1/8"
FRONT LEG

1/4" x 7/8" x 3 3/16"
JAW

1 SQUARE = 1/2"

5. Using your drill and a 1-1/4" hole saw with 1/4" guide bit, cut four 3/4" x 1-1/4"-diameter Type A wheels (see page 37).

6. Bore a 9/32" through-hole in each axle support (see page 38). Center each hole between the 1-1/4" faces, 1/2" from either 3/4" edge of the support, so that the tops of the wheels don't touch the bottom of the pond.

7. Using a 9/32" twist-drill bit, bore a 1/8"-deep depression at the eye and nostril marks on both sides of the body.

8. Carefully rasp and sand the tool marks and rough spots from all parts and round the axle ends completely.

9. Secure the body upside down and, using the body pattern as a guide, lay out a centered, 5/16"-wide, 3-1/8"-long slot for the counterbalance on the bottom of the neck.

10. To remove most of the wood from the slot, use a 1/4" bradpoint bit to bore closely spaced holes, each 1-1/8" deep, between the marked slot lines.

11. Remove the remaining waste with a paring or firmer chisel, taking care not to split the thin cheeks. Check the depth and width of the slot frequently. Paring is a skill requiring patience and dexterity rather than strength, so easy does it!

12. Glue and clamp the two jaws onto the counterbalance. When the assembly is dry, test-fit it in the slot. If any parts fail to mate neatly with their opposing parts, trim them as necessary with a coping saw or chisel. (The "wobble-action" jaw won't function unless there's plenty of clearance around the counterbalance.)

13. To fasten the jaw assembly to the body, first dimple the site of the pivot hole on the face of the cheek.

14. Hold the counterbalance in place within the slot. Then use a 1/16" twist-drill bit to carefully bore a hole straight through the dimpled cheek, the counterbalance, and the opposite cheek. Set the jaw assembly aside.

15. Glue and clamp the front and back leg pairs to the body. Before the glue sets up, set the assembly on a flat surface and adjust the leg positions until the feet rest flat. Set the assembly aside to dry.

16. Using your pilot bit, bore the four pilot holes for the axle supports on the top face of the pond piece.

17. Locate the 3/4" edges of the axle supports that are farthest from the 9/32" through-holes. Place these edges onto the bottom of the pond so that the inside faces of the supports are 9-1/2" apart and the outer face of the rear support is 2-1/4" from the curved back edge of the pond. Use a straightedge to check that the ends of the supports are aligned. Then drive four 1" deck screws through the pilot holes and into the supports.

18. To fasten the gator and log to the pond, first double-check that the gator's feet match the pilot-hole layouts on the pond's bottom face by placing the gator onto the pond's opposite surface and checking the alignment with your tape measure. Adjust the layout as necessary; then bore the four pilot holes.

19. Use your imagination and available finishing materials to create an appealing environment for your gator. Artist's acrylic colors work well. Use 200-grit sandpaper and very light pressure to scrub off any wood grain that's raised by the water-based paint. To create bubbles and ripples on the pond, scratch the paint while it's still wet. Protect the painted surfaces by finishing them with a coat of water-based satin varnish. Finish the wheels and axles with satin varnish only; this transparent finish on the "transport parts" allows the colorful gator to take center stage.

20. Glue the lily pads in place on the pond's top face. When the glue has dried, secure the pads by carefully driving a 1/2" brad through the pond's bottom face and into each one. (Avoid driving the brads completely, or they may protrude slightly from the top surfaces of the pads.)

21. Place the log and gator on the pond, aligning the gator carefully with the pilot holes in the pond's bottom face. Clamp the three pieces together lightly. With your pilot bit, complete the holes through the log and into the gator's feet.

22. Attach the log and gator to the pond with four 1" deck screws.

23. Insert the axles through the axle supports and secure the wheels to the axles with No. 18 x 5/8" brads (see page 39).

24. Adjusting the counterbalanced jaw assembly is an exercise in fine motor control! Begin by marking a 1-3/4" length of 1/4" threaded rod, carriage bolt, or hex-head bolt and cutting it with your hacksaw.

25. Mix up about a teaspoonful of quick-setting epoxy. Then spread a 1/16"-thick layer along the section of the counterbalance's flat (upper) edge that is opposite to the section surrounded by teeth. While the epoxy sets up to a sticky consistency (several minutes at most), set two flat-topped objects of equal size approximately 1" apart on your work surface; wood blocks or paint cans will work well.

26. Slide your 1/32" twist-drill bit through the pivot hole in the jaw. Then set the two ends of the drill bit onto the blocks or cans so that the jaw rests freely between them. The toothed end of the jaw will drop down. Gently center the piece of threaded rod above the width and length of the gluey edge section and press it into the sticky epoxy. Slide the rod carefully back and forth until the jaw rests level or rocks gently back and forth. Let the glue dry thoroughly.

27. With your wire-cutting pliers, cut a 3/4" pivot pin from a 3d finishing nail. (Discard the head of the nail.) Lightly file the ends of the pin flat.

28. Mix a few drops of epoxy together. Place a small drop into one pivot hole only, set the jaw assembly in place, and press or drive the pivot pin into the pivot hole that's without glue and then on through until it is glued in place; its ends should be hidden from little fingers. Place another drop of epoxy on each end of the pivot to further secure the pin. The jaw will now bob freely in its slot. Creepy!

29. Complete your Hungry Gator by boring a centered 1/16" hole, 1/2" deep, into the front edge of the pond piece; use a 1/16" bit flagged for a 1/2" boring depth. Insert the screw eye, attach the cord to it, and you're all set for gift-giving.

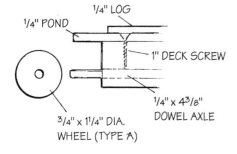

1/4" POND
1/4" LOG
1" DECK SCREW
1/4" x 4³/8" DOWEL AXLE
3/4" x 1¹/4" DIA. WHEEL (TYPE A)

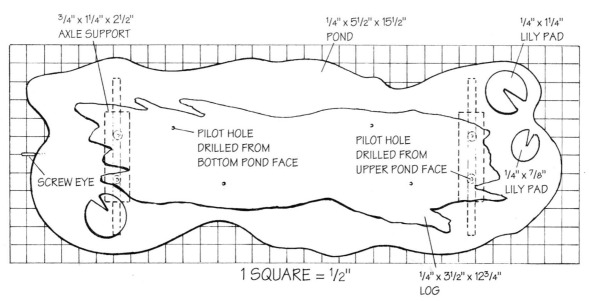

3/4" x 1¹/4" x 2¹/2" AXLE SUPPORT

1/4" x 5¹/2" x 15¹/2" POND

1/4" x 1¹/4" LILY PAD

PILOT HOLE DRILLED FROM BOTTOM POND FACE

PILOT HOLE DRILLED FROM UPPER POND FACE

1/4" x 7/8" LILY PAD

SCREW EYE

1 SQUARE = 1/2"

1/4" x 3¹/2" x 12³/4" LOG

TURTLE DOVE

• • • •

*These two best friends may soon
be your child's as well.*

CUT LIST

1 Figure • 3/4" x 6-1/4" x 10"
1 Base • 3/4" x 3-1/2" x 9"
2 Legs • 3/8" x 2-3/4" dowel
2 Axles • 1/4" x 5-3/8" dowel
4 Wheels (Type A) • 3/4" x 1-3/8"-diameter

HARDWARE AND SUPPLIES

4 No. 18 x 3/4" brads
5 Size 112 small screw eyes
1 36" length of decorative cord

SUGGESTED TOOLS

Layout tools
Backsaw and miter box
Circular saw
Jigsaw with scrolling blade
Rasps
Claw hammer
3/8" drill
1/16" and 3/8" twist-drill bits
1-3/8" hole saw with 1/4" guide bit
Pad sander

TIPS

• *You'll find a selection of decorative cord at your
local fabric outlet.*

• *A short scrap of 1/4" dowel can serve as a useful
tool for tightening screw eyes. Just slip the dowel
into the eye and use it as a lever for turning.*

INSTRUCTIONS

1. Enlarge the cutting pattern for the figure and transfer it onto 3/4" stock.

2. Cut the figure out with your jigsaw and scrolling blade, using your 3/8" twist-drill bit to start a hole for the interior cuts.

3. Secure the figure, upside down, to your work surface. To indicate the boring angles for the 3/8" leg holes, mark a line for each one on one face of the figure.

4. Using a 3/8" bit stopped for a 1/2" depth, carefully bore the two leg holes in the edge of the figure.

5. Lay out the 3-1/2" x 9" base on 3/4" stock and cut it out with your circular saw.

6. In the upper face of the base, mark and bore two angled 3/8" leg holes to 1/2" depths; center these holes across the base's width, 3" and 5" from the base's front edge.

7. On the bottom face of the base, mark four boring locations for the axle screw eyes. Locate each hole 1-1/8" from an end and 3/8" from an edge. Also mark a location for the cord's screw eye, centering it on the front end of the base.

8. With a 1/16" twist-drill bit flagged for a 1/2" depth, bore the five holes for the screw eyes.

9. Use your backsaw to cut the two 3/8" dowel legs to 2-3/4" in length and the two 1/4" dowel axles to 5-3/8" in length.

10. Cut four 1-3/8"-diameter Type A wheels from 3/4" stock (see page 37).

11. Round the ends of the axles with your flat rasp and sandpaper. To remove tool marks and ease all arrises, rasp and sand all the remaining parts.

12. Prime all parts with latex primer. Let them dry thoroughly and sand them lightly.

13. Finish the parts with a faux finish (see page 58) and allow them to dry completely.

14. Glue the two dowel legs into the base, driving them into place with your hammer. Then glue the legs' top ends into the holes in the figure's bottom edge.

15. Install the four screw eyes in the four holes in the bottom of the base, turning them so that their open eyes are parallel to the long edges of the base.

16. Slip the axles through the pairs of screw eyes. Place the wheels onto the ends of the axles, leaving a 1/16" space between the inside face of each wheel and the edge of the base. (If the axles don't turn easily, use a pair of slip-joint pliers to open the screw eyes slightly.)

17. Secure the wheels to the axles with No. 18 x 3/4" brads (see page 39).

18. Install the fifth screw eye into the front end of the base, tie the decorative cord to it, and you're ready to surprise a young friend!

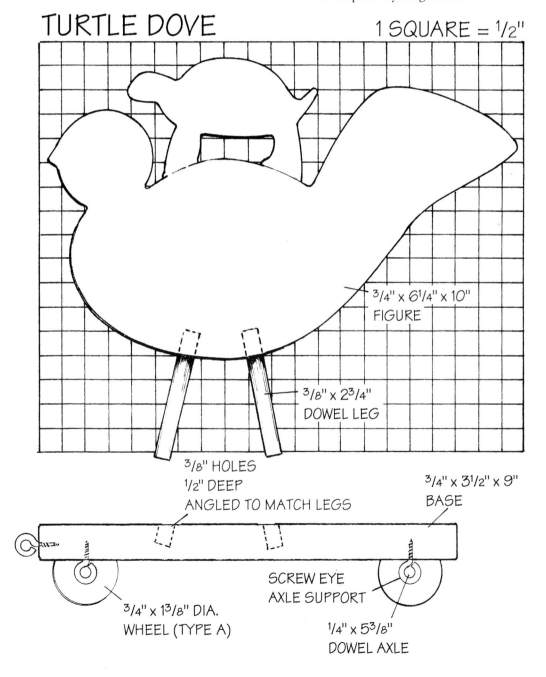

TURTLE DOVE   1 SQUARE = 1/2"

3/4" x 6 1/4" x 10"
FIGURE

3/8" x 2 3/4"
DOWEL LEG

3/8" HOLES
1/2" DEEP
ANGLED TO MATCH LEGS

3/4" x 3 1/2" x 9"
BASE

SCREW EYE
AXLE SUPPORT

3/4" x 1 3/8" DIA.
WHEEL (TYPE A)

1/4" x 5 3/8"
DOWEL AXLE

TWIG DRAGON

••••

*Here's an easy project that's perfect for
an adult and child to build together.*

CUT LIST

1 Base • 3/4" x 7-1/4" x 14"
4 Wheels (Type A) • 3/4" x 1-3/8"-diameter
2 Axles • 1/4" x 7-1/2" dowel
1 Dragon (see Step 1) • 14" twig

HARDWARE AND SUPPLIES

4 1-1/4" deck screws
4 No. 18 x 3/4" brads
4 Size 112 small screw eyes

SUGGESTED TOOLS

Layout tools
Backsaw and miter box
Coping saw
Circular saw
Claw hammer
No. 2 Phillips screwdriver
3/8" drill
1/32", 1/16", and 1/8" twist-drill bits
Pilot bit for 1-1/4" deck screws
Counterbore to match deck-screw head size
1-3/8" hole saw with 1/4" guide bit
Pad sander

INSTRUCTIONS

1. Take your youngster on a dragon hunt! Look for a dead branch, about 14" long, with limbs that suggest the shape of a dragon. A three-or five-legged dragon is fine, but the "legs" should point in the same general direction so that they'll fasten easily to the base piece, and each leg should be at least 3/8" thick. The "feet" should fit onto the base piece with room to spare. If they don't—and you really like the dragon you've captured—adjust the width and length of the base and axles to fit the dragon's size.

2. Lay out and cut to size the base piece and the two axles.

3. Use your drill with a 1-3/8" hole saw with 1/4" guide bit to cut four 1-3/8"-diameter Type A wheels (see page 37).

4. Position the dragon on the top face of the base and, if necessary, use a coping saw to trim its feet until they rest flat. Mark the location of each foot.

5. At the center of each leg location, bore a 1/8" hole through the face of the base.

6. Flip the base over and counterbore each hole with a counterbore that fits your 1-1/4" deck screws.

7. Sand all parts carefully, rounding the ends of the axles. Then remove the sanding dust.

8. Finish all parts, including the dragon, with a transparent finish, letting each coat dry thoroughly and sanding lightly between coats. Add painted eyes or other details as you wish.

9. Turn the base so that the counterbores face up. Now lay out four bore holes for the screw eyes, 15/16" from each edge and 1-1/2" from each end.

10. At each mark, bore a 1/16" pilot hole, 1/2" deep.

11. Install the screw eyes in the holes, aligning their eyes parallel with the edges of the base.

12. Fasten the dragon's feet to the base with 1-1/4" deck screws. (You may need to bore pilot holes in the feet to keep them from splitting when you drive the screws.)

13. Slide the axles through the pairs of screw eyes and slip wheels onto their ends, allowing the axles' ends to project 1/4" from the wheels' outer faces. Secure the wheels with brads (see page 39).

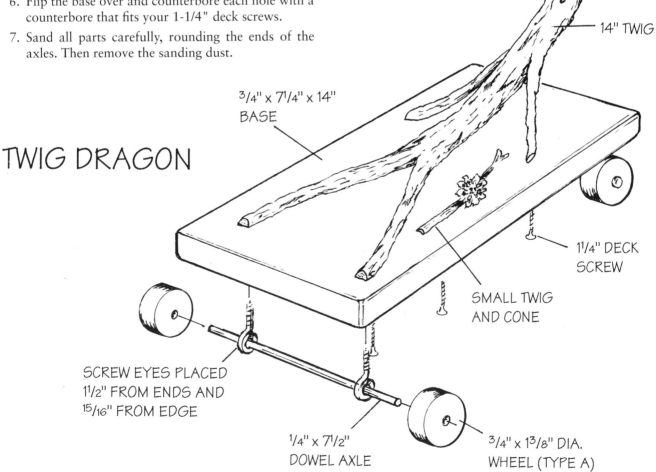

TWIG DRAGON

3/4" x 7¹/4" x 14" BASE

14" TWIG

1¹/4" DECK SCREW

SMALL TWIG AND CONE

SCREW EYES PLACED 1¹/2" FROM ENDS AND ¹⁵/16" FROM EDGE

1/4" x 7¹/2" DOWEL AXLE

3/4" x 1³/8" DIA. WHEEL (TYPE A)

BOB'S SLED

•••••

Inspired by an antique tin toy, this heirloom design will keep your kids smiling when the winter weather has driven them indoors.

CUT LIST

- 1 Figure • 3/4" x 3" x 8"
- 2 Arms • 1/4" x 1-3/8" x 2-5/8"
- 2 Runners • 1/4" x 2" x 9"
- 2 Braces • 1/4" x 3/4" x 2-1/4"
- 1 Deck • 1/4" x 2-1/4" x 7-1/4"
- 1 Hand grip • 1/4" x 2-1/2" dowel
- 2 Axles • 1/4" x 3" dowel
- 4 Wheels (Type A) • 1/4" x 1-1/4"-diameter

HARDWARE AND SUPPLIES

- 2 1" deck screws
- 4 No. 18 x 5/8" brads
- 8 No. 18 x 3/4" wire nails

TIP

- *The small scale of Bob's Sled makes it perfect for using up small scrap pieces left over from other projects.*

SUGGESTED TOOLS

Layout tools
Backsaw and miter box
Circular saw
Jigsaw with scrolling blade
Rasps
Claw hammer
No. 2 Phillips screwdriver
3/8" drill
1/4" bradpoint bit
1/32" and 9/32" twist-drill bits
Pilot bit for 1" deck screws
1-1/4" hole saw with 1/4" guide bit
Pad sander

INSTRUCTIONS

1. Enlarge the cutting patterns and transfer them onto lumber of appropriate thickness (see "Cut List"). Also transfer the hole locations in the runners.

2. Cut out the shapes—and the deck—with your jigsaw and scrolling blade and your circular saw. To start the interior cutouts in the runners, first bore 1/4" holes through them to allow access for your jigsaw blade.

3. On the inside face of each runner, bore the four 1/32" nail holes, two 9/32" axle holes, and one 1/4" hand-grip hole, 1/8" deep.

4. Referring to the runner pattern, mark and bore two deck-screw pilot holes through one face of the deck, centering them across the deck's width. Screws inserted through these holes will fasten the figure in place.

5. With your backsaw and miter box, cut the 2-1/2" dowel hand grip and the two 3" dowel axles to length.

6. Use your rasps and sandpaper to remove tool marks and rough spots from all parts and to round and smooth the square ends of the deck and the ends of the hand grip and axles. With sandpaper, ease the arrises of the figure, the arms, the runners, and the braces.

7. Using your drill and a 1-1/4" hole saw with 1/4" guide bit, cut four 1-1/4"-diameter Type A wheels from 1/4" stock (see page 37). Sand them well.

8. Glue and clamp the two arms onto the figure. When the arms are joined properly and the figure's stomach is placed on a flat surface, the forearms will also rest lightly on that surface.

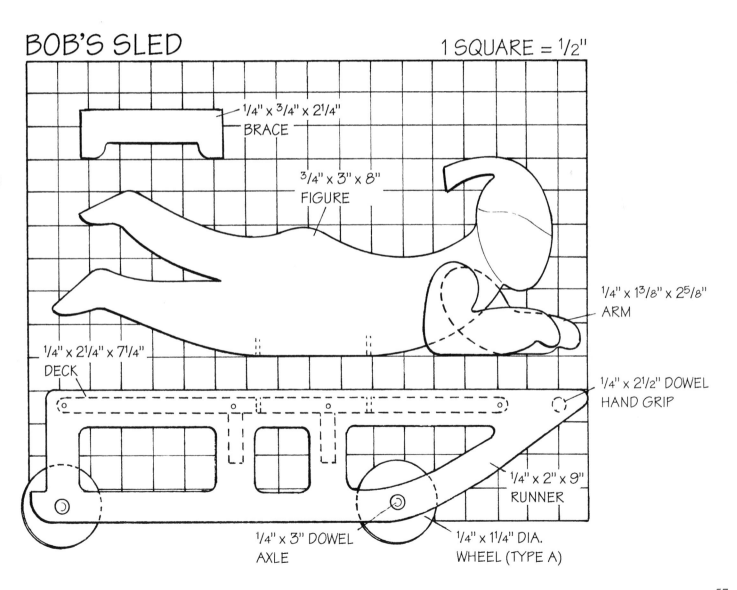

BOB'S SLED 1 SQUARE = 1/2"

1/4" x 3/4" x 2 1/4" BRACE

3/4" x 3" x 8" FIGURE

1/4" x 1 3/8" x 2 5/8" ARM

1/4" x 2 1/4" x 7 1/4" DECK

1/4" x 2 1/2" DOWEL HAND GRIP

1/4" x 2" x 9" RUNNER

1/4" x 3" DOWEL AXLE

1/4" x 1 1/4" DIA. WHEEL (TYPE A)

9. Prime all parts except the deck with latex primer. Let the parts dry thoroughly; then sand them lightly to further smooth their surfaces.

10. This is an ideal project for a faux finish (see below). For the best possible job, finish each part separately before assembly. Allow the paint to dry.

11. Attach one runner to one long edge of the deck, using wire nails driven through the four 1/32" holes.

12. To secure the hand grip and second runner, first apply a small drop of glue to both 1/4" hand-grip holes in the runners. Then position the hand grip in the gluey holes before attaching the second runner onto the opposite edge of the deck.

13. Glue the two braces in place beneath the deck and between the runners.

14. Fasten the figure onto the deck with two 1" deck screws inserted through the pilot holes.

15. Slide the axles through the 9/32" through-holes in one runner. Slip two wheels over the inner portion of each axle before sliding the axle on through the opposing hole in the other runner. Space each wheel so that its outer face is 1/16" from the inner face of a runner; an equal length of axle should protrude from each runner.

16. Use brads to secure the wheels permanently to the axles (see page 39).

17. If Bob's Sled still looks suspiciously new, age it a bit further with sandpaper and rasps or give it to your younger children. They'll give it a genuine antique look in no time!

faux fun

Faux (false) finishes are usually applied in an attempt to make an object look older, rarer, or more valuable than it is. In this book, they're most often used to enhance the visual and tactile qualities of the projects and to remind us of toys from days gone by. Any plaything will age rapidly in the hands of a young owner, so think of your faux painting as a step towards the inevitable!

Projects with nostalgic designs tend to wear their faux "clothes" more comfortably than contemporary projects, so consider your project's design lines before selecting materials and colors. Also keep in mind that flat or semigloss paints in muted colors don't scream "new" as brilliant gloss finishes do.

For inspiration on color combinations and detailing, visit a toy museum or browse through collectors' books; the latter are often loaded with color photos of antique toys. Whether the photographed toys are fashioned from lead, tin, wood, or paper, what you'll be looking for are pleasingly petrified colors that you can reproduce in your shop by mixing paints. Keep in mind that combining faux-finished parts with unfinished parts can be highly effective.

Bob's Sled offers a good example of an easily mastered faux-finishing method. To replicate it, first brush on primer, straight from the can. (The mousy, gray-green primer color provides a neutral backdrop for colors to come.) Then use vermillion, violet, green, a flesh tone, and a silvery finish to delineate the various project parts; to subdue these colors, add a drop or two of black to each. Note that the color areas are simplified, and colors are not mixed within shapes. For detail work, use round or flat brushes in smaller sizes such as Nos. 1 and 2. White, black, and metallic paints are effective if they aren't overused.

After the paint has dried thoroughly, gently rub the surfaces here and there with a well-used scrap of 220-grit sandpaper or 0000 steel wool. Your goal is to remove the finish where a child's fingers might naturally have abraded it. Gradually reveal the paint and wood. To add detail, use an awl to scrape and dimple the surface lightly.

When you've aged the project to your satisfaction, remove any debris and apply varnish, which will help protect the project without ruining the visual effect of the damaged finish.

BED BUG

•••••

This bouncy beetle's ready to spring from its bunk straight into your child's heart.

CUT LIST

1 Mattress • 1-1/2" x 4-3/4" x 7"
1 Headboard • 3/4" x 5-1/2" x 6"
1 Footboard • 3/4" x 5-1/2" x 4-3/4"
1 Body • 3/4" x 3" x 3-3/4"
1 Wings • 1/4" x 3-1/2" x 4"
1 Head • 3/4" x 2-3/4"-diameter
8 Legs and antennae • 1/4" x 1-3/4" dowel
4 Wheels (Type A) • 1/4" x 1-3/8"-diameter
4 Axles • 1/4" x 3/4" dowel

HARDWARE AND SUPPLIES

5 1-5/8" deck screws
4 No. 18 x 3/4" brads
6 No. 18 x 3/4" wire nails
1 Size 112 small screw eye
1 1/2" x 3-1/4" spring
1 10" x 20" piece fabric
  Thread to match fabric
  Polyester batting
1 36" length of braided cord
  Quick-setting epoxy resin glue

SUGGESTED TOOLS

Layout tools
Backsaw and miter box
Circular saw
Coping saw
Jigsaw with medium-toothed and scrolling blades
Rasps
Claw hammer
No. 2 Phillips screwdriver
3/8" drill
1/16" twist-drill bit
1/4" and 1/2" bradpoint bits
Pilot bit for 1-5/8" deck screws
1-3/8" hole saw with 1/4" guide bit
Pad sander
Needle

TIP

• *If you can't find the right spring at a hardware store, check to see if there's an industrial outlet in town that sells a variety of springs.*

INSTRUCTIONS

1. Mark and cut the mattress, headboard, and footboard to the rough sizes provided in the "Cut List."

2. Enlarge all the cutting patterns and transfer those for the body, wings, and head to the appropriate stock. (Also transfer the accompanying hole locations.) Cut these three pieces out, using your circular saw and jigsaw; don't shape the headboard and footboard pieces just yet.

3. Cut the four Type A wheels from 1/4" stock, using your 1-3/8" hole saw with 1/4" guide bit (see page 37).

4. Using the patterns as guides, mark locations for the four 1/4" axle holes on the edges of the headboard and footboard pieces. Each hole is 3/8" across an edge and 1/2" from an end.

5. At each mark, use your 1/4" bradpoint bit to bore a 1"-deep hole.

6. Transfer the headboard and footboard patterns, along with their pilot-hole locations, and cut the shapes out with your jigsaw and medium-toothed blade. Finish cross-grain cuts in the wheel slots with your coping saw.

7. On the upper face of the mattress piece, mark one 1/2" hole, centering it across the piece's width, 4" from one end. With your 1/2" bit, bore the 1"-deep hole.

8. On the bottom face of the body, bore the 1/2" spring hole to a 1/2" depth.

9. On the same face, bore the pilot hole for the 1-5/8" deck screw.

10. Using your 1/4" bradpoint bit, bore the six 1/4" leg holes in the body. Each hole is centered on the edge and is 3/4" deep.

11. In the head piece, bore two 1/4" holes, each 3/4" deep, for the angled antennae. The 45-degree angles of these holes aren't critical, but try to make the two angles identical. Using the same bit, bore 1/8"-deep indentations for the eyes.

12. With your backsaw and miter box, cut the eight 1/4" antennae and legs to 1-3/4" in length.

13. Use your hacksaw to cut the 1/2" spring to 3-1/4" in length.

14. Carefully rasp and sand all wooden parts to remove tool marks and ease all arrises.

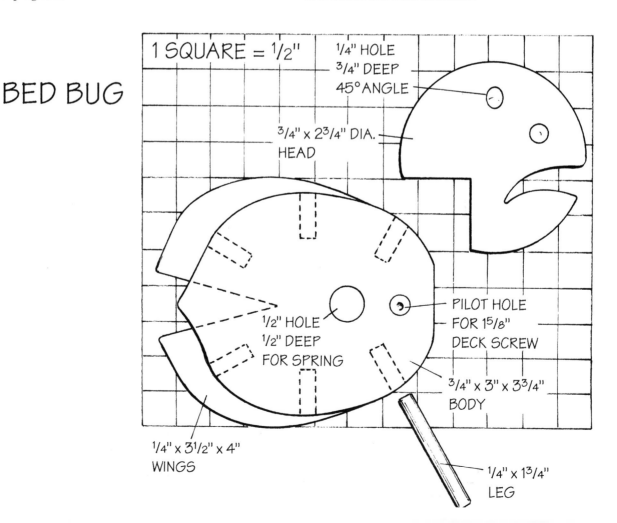

1 SQUARE = 1/2"

BED BUG

1/4" HOLE
3/4" DEEP
45° ANGLE

3/4" x 2 3/4" DIA.
HEAD

1/2" HOLE
1/2" DEEP
FOR SPRING

PILOT HOLE
FOR 1 5/8"
DECK SCREW

3/4" x 3" x 3 3/4"
BODY

1/4" x 3 1/2" x 4"
WINGS

1/4" x 1 3/4"
LEG

15. Finish the parts to suit your taste. Our bug is finished in black and pastel artist's acrylic colors. The bed has two coats of water-based varnish on it. (The bug also has a couple of coats of the same finish to protect it from wear.)

16. Secure the head to the body with a 1-5/8" deck screw driven through the pilot hole in the body. Attach the legs and antennae by using a drop or two of glue in each hole. Leave the spring unattached for now.

17. Secure the mattress to the headboard and footboard with four 1-5/8" deck screws inserted through the pairs of pilot holes; align the bottom edge of the mattress with the bottom edges of the C-shaped cutouts in the headboard and footboard.

18. Assemble the wheel parts in their axle holes. Glue the axles in the holes, but leave the wheels unglued so that they'll spin freely. To further secure the axles, drive a brad through the face of the headboard/footboard and into the axle at each of the four axle locations.

19. Fold the quilt fabric in half. Then stitch the edges and all but a few inches of one side together. Fill the quilt with batting, sew the quilt closed, and work the material with your fingers to spread the batting evenly throughout.

20. Time to make the bed! Place the quilt on the mattress, folding it at one end to create a pillow shape. Then drive three evenly spaced wire nails through the quilt and into each edge of the mattress. (Use one nail on each edge to secure the pillow shape.)

21. Probing through the quilt, locate the 1/2" hole in the mattress face. With your utility knife, carefully make a 3/4" slit through the quilt at that point.

22. Mix up a small amount of epoxy. Spread the quilt fabric and batting to expose the mattress hole and place about six to eight drops of epoxy in the hole. Then press one end of the spring into it. Also apply glue to the 1/2" hole in the body and attach the body to the spring's top end. Before the glue sets up, align the body so that it faces the footboard.

23. In the footboard, mark and bore a 1/16" pilot hole for the screw eye. Insert the screw eye and tie on the braided cord. You're all set!

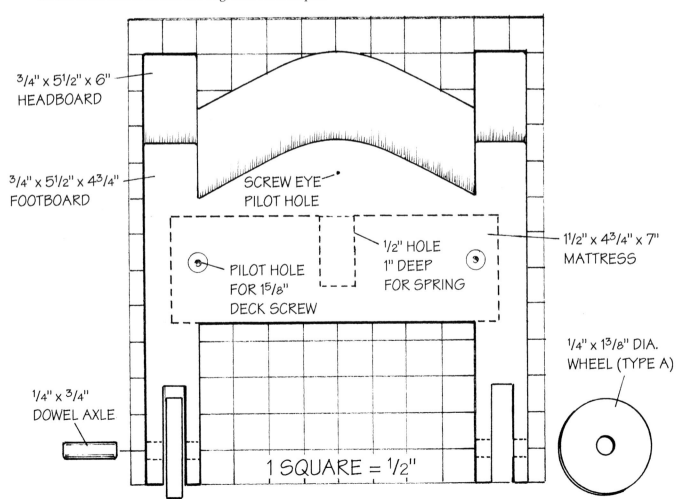

3/4" x 5 1/2" x 6" HEADBOARD

3/4" x 5 1/2" x 4 3/4" FOOTBOARD

SCREW EYE PILOT HOLE

PILOT HOLE FOR 1 5/8" DECK SCREW

1/2" HOLE 1" DEEP FOR SPRING

1 1/2" x 4 3/4" x 7" MATTRESS

1/4" x 1 3/8" DIA. WHEEL (TYPE A)

1/4" x 3/4" DOWEL AXLE

1 SQUARE = 1/2"

PUZZLE TRUCK

••••

Kids love puzzles, and what could be more fun than six different puzzles in a custom truck?

CUT LIST

- 1 Bed • 3/4" x 7-1/4" x 7-1/4"
- 2 Long sides • 3/4" x 2" x 6-1/2"
- 2 Short sides • 3/4" x 2" x 5"
- 1 Cab • 1-1/2" x 5-1/2" x 7-1/4"
- 1 Hood • 1-1/2" x 3" x 7-1/4"
- 1 Bumper • 3/4" x 1-1/2" x 7-1/4"
- 2 Skirts • 3/4" x 1" x 8-3/4"
- 4 Wheels (Type A) • 3/4" x 2-3/4"-diameter
- 2 Axles • 3/8" x 9-3/8" dowel
- 4 Lights • 1/2" x 1" dowel
- 4 Cubes • 2-1/4" x 2-1/4" x 2-1/4"
- 1 Antenna • 3/8" x 2-1/2" dowel

HARDWARE AND SUPPLIES

- 4 1" deck screws
- 24 1-1/4" deck screws
- 4 6d finishing nails
  Magazine illustrations, optional

SUGGESTED TOOLS

Layout tools
Backsaw and miter box
Circular saw
Jigsaw with scrolling blade
Rasps
Claw hammer
No. 2 Phillips screwdriver
3/8" drill
3/8" bradpoint bit
13/32" twist-drill bit
1-1/4" Forstner bit
Pilot bits for 1" and 1-1/4" deck screws
Router with 3/8" rounding-over bit
Pad sander

TIPS

- *The 1-1/2"-thick cab and hood parts of this project can be glued up from two pieces of 3/4"-thick stock. Glued-up stock can be treated exactly like thicker stock and is easy to create from thinner scraps.*

- *Use extra caution when cutting small parts such as the blocks.*

INSTRUCTIONS

1. Using your circular saw and referring to the "Cut List," mark and cut the various flat parts (excluding the wheels) to size.

2. Mark and cut the dowels to length, using your backsaw and miter box.

3. Mark and cut out the four 2-3/4"-diameter Type A wheels (see page 37). Then bore a centered 3/8" through-hole in each one.

4. With your compass, mark 1/2" radii on the rear corners of the bed piece, on the bottom corners of each skirt piece, and on the two front corners of the bumper.

5. Saw the radii with your jigsaw and scrolling blade.

6. Mark the arrises of the cab and hood parts for routing, as shown in the diagram. Secure the parts carefully and round the marked arrises with the 3/8" rounding-over bit.

7. Three of the side pieces have semicircles cut in their upper edges; these make it easier for little fingers to grasp the puzzle blocks. To create these cutouts, first align and clamp the two long sides together, edge to edge. Then clamp the paired pieces face up on your work surface, with scrap wood beneath them. Along the joint line between the two pieces, make a mark 3-1/4" from either end. Bore through the mark, using a 1-1/4" Forstner bit; the bit will cut a semicircular shape from the edge of each piece.

8. Repeat Step 7 on one edge of one short side piece, clamping a 3/4"-thick scrap with it as a replacement for the other short side piece and measuring only 2-1/2" from either end. (The remaining short side piece, which will face the cab, doesn't require a cutout.)

9. Mark and bore a 3/8" antenna hole, 3/4" deep, in the upper edge of the hood piece, 1" from the edge and 1" from the rounded front face.

10. With your rasps, remove the rough tool marks; also round the ends of the axle dowels and one end of the antenna.

11. In the face of each long side piece, mark and bore four pilot holes for 1-1/4" deck screws; locate each hole 3/8" from an end and 3/8" from an edge.

12. Spread a bit of glue on the ends of the short side pieces. Then position the two long side pieces on them to form a 6-1/2"-square box shape. Secure the pieces with 1-1/4" deck screws inserted in the pilot holes.

13. Set the bed face down. Using your adjustable square, mark two lines, each 3/4" from an edge, along the board. Then, measuring from the bed's square end, mark each line at 1", 3-1/4", and 5-1/2", and bore a pilot hole for a 1-1/4" deck screw at each location.

14. Turn the assembled box shape so that the semicircles face down. Run a line of glue around the edges that face up and carefully set the bed onto the gluey edges so that the bed's square end is aligned with the outside face of the short side piece that has no cutout. The bed should overlap the two long side pieces by 3/8" on each side. To secure the assembly, drive 1-1/4" deck screws through the pilot holes.

15. Spread some glue on the square face of the hood and then place that face onto the portion of the cab's face that hasn't been routed. Before clamping the parts together, carefully align the pieces' bottom edges and ends.

16. While the cab-and-hood assembly is drying, mark and bore two 13/32" axle holes through the face of each skirt, 1-1/4" from each end and centered across the face.

17. Turn the skirt pieces so that the flat edges are face down. Lay out and bore two pilot holes for 1-1/4" deck screws in each piece's rounded face, centering each hole across the edge, 1-3/4" from an end.

18. Place the bed-and-box assembly on its square end. On the inside face of the lower short side, lay out four pilot holes, each 1/2" from an edge and an end. Bore pilot holes for 1-1/4" deck screws at these locations.

19. Spread some glue onto the surface of the bed-and-box assembly that has no cutout in it. Then clamp the gluey surface to the face of the cab-and-hood assembly. Deep-jawed clamps such as large C-clamps are effective for this job.

20. To secure the pieces, drive four 1-1/4" deck screws through the pilot holes in the short side piece.

PUZZLE TRUCK

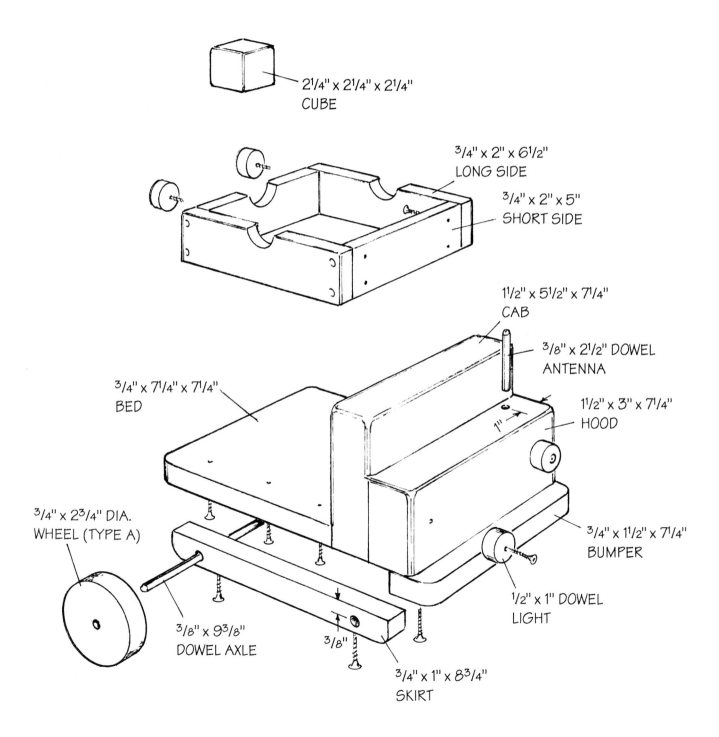

$2^1/4$" x $2^1/4$" x $2^1/4$"
CUBE

$3/4$" x 2" x $6^1/2$"
LONG SIDE

$3/4$" x 2" x 5"
SHORT SIDE

$1^1/2$" x $5^1/2$" x $7^1/4$"
CAB

$3/8$" x $2^1/2$" DOWEL
ANTENNA

$3/4$" x $7^1/4$" x $7^1/4$"
BED

$1^1/2$" x 3" x $7^1/4$"
HOOD

1"

$3/4$" x $2^3/4$" DIA.
WHEEL (TYPE A)

$3/4$" x $1^1/2$" x $7^1/4$"
BUMPER

$3/8$" x $9^3/8$"
DOWEL AXLE

$3/8$"

$1/2$" x 1" DOWEL
LIGHT

$3/4$" x 1" x $8^3/4$"
SKIRT

21. Turn the assembly upside down. Spread a line of glue along the flat face of each skirt piece. Then place the skirts onto the bed so that their outside faces align with the edges of the bed and their back ends are 3/4" from the bed's rounded end. To fasten the skirts, drive four 1-1/4" deck screws into their pilot holes.

22. Glue the dowel antenna into the 3/8" hole in the hood, driving it in with your hammer if necessary.

23. With a center finder, locate and mark the center of each dowel light piece. Then clamp each light to your work surface with a piece of scrap wood beneath it and bore a pilot hole through it for a 1" deck screw.

24. Fasten one pair of lights onto the hood's face and the other onto the outside face of the short side piece at the rear of the truck. Use 1" deck screws to attach the rear lights, placing the lights 3/4" from the short side's ends and 3/4" from its bottom edge. Fasten the front lights in a similar fashion, 1" from the rounded ends of the hood and 1-3/4" from its square edge.

25. Set the bumper with one face up. Mark and bore two pilot holes for 1-1/4" screws, 1" from the rounded ends and 3/8" from the square edge.

26. Turn the Puzzle Truck upside down again. Apply a line of glue (from pilot hole to pilot hole) to the face of the bumper that is opposite to its counterbores. Butt that face against the flat bottom of the hood, with its rounded edge facing out. Press the pieces together so that the bumper's square edge fits tightly against the rounded ends of the skirt pieces. Align the bumper's ends with the hood's edges and drive two 1-1/4" deck screws through the pilot holes.

27. Sand all parts carefully, including the blocks, wheels, and axles. Smooth all arrises well.

28. Slip the axles through the holes in the skirts and slide the wheels on until a 1/16" gap remains between their inside faces and the sides of the truck. Fasten the wheels to the axles with finishing nails (see page 39).

29. Finish the Puzzle Truck itself (but not the blocks) with a transparent finish such as water-based varnish, which will highlight the colorful blocks. Apply two or more coats, according to the manufacturer's directions. For suggestions on finishing the block set, read on!

a perfect puzzle

Finishing the blocks for the Puzzle Truck calls for a bit of planning. First, to plan puzzles that are age appropriate, consider the kids who will use them. A simple color-matching or shape-matching puzzle is fine for two- and three-year-olds; a numbers puzzle or complex pattern puzzle is better suited for older children.

Painting the blocks with latex enamel paints in bright, contrasting colors—a different color for each set of puzzle surfaces—is an ideal approach for toddlers. Basic shape sets such as circles, rectangles, and triangles help older preschoolers learn more about concepts of identical and differing images; mixing up the background colors with the shapes adds another step in complexity.

Block sets with animal themes—circuses, farms, and wildlife—are great choices, too. Ask your children what their favorite animals are; they'll design the block set for you!

Letter sets, number sets, and patterns of dots will challenge children who are learning to recognize the alphabet or studying basic counting concepts. Consider multiple dot or shape patterns, including color variants for added interest. A set of blocks featuring faces with colored dots numbered one through twenty-four may start your counting kids on a short track to the Nobel Prize in mathematics or at least provide them with hours of counting and matching fun in the meantime! Make your patterns big, bold, and clearly legible.

Picture puzzles are a wonderful variation and may remind older builders of the fancifully decorated puzzles that they grew up with years ago. Here, the same general rules apply. From magazines or other sources, select illustrations that feature simplified graphics and bright, contrasting colors. Cut the illustrations into four 2-1/4" x 2-1/4" squares and glue them onto the blocks' faces with rubber cement. Finishing the faces with a coat or two of water-based varnish will help protect them from wear and tear. A well-made picture-puzzle set featuring six different pictures will challenge the most enterprising kids and even some adults!

PLATO THE PLATYPUS

• • • •

*Its flapping flippers and floppy tail make this
strange little creature a hit with your kids.*

CUT LIST

1 Body • 3/4" x 5-3/4" x 16-1/2"
2 Mouth sides • 1/4" x 2-3/4" x 3-3/8"
1 Tail • 1/4" x 2-11/16" x 7-3/4"
2 Front legs • 1/4" x 3-1/4" x 5-1/16"
2 Rear legs • 1/4" x 3" x 3-7/8"
4 Wheels (Type A) • 3/4" x 3-3/8"-diameter
4 Axles • 3/8" x 3-1/2" dowel
1 Push stick • 1/2" x 31-1/2" dowel
1 Push-stick handle • 1-1/2" x 1-1/2" x 2"

HARDWARE AND SUPPLIES

1 1-1/4" deck screw
2 3/16" cut washers
4 3/8" cut washers
8 4d finishing nails
4 6d finishing nails
1 Rubber stair-tread cover

Layout tools
Backsaw and miter box
Circular saw
Jigsaw with scrolling blade
Rasps
Claw hammer
No. 2 Phillips screwdriver
3/8" drill
1/8", 3/8", 7/16", and 1/2" bradpoint bits
1/16" and 3/64" twist-drill bits
Pad sander

TIPS

- *Purchase the stair-tread covers at a hardware store or floor-covering shop.*
- *If 1/4"-thick solid stock is unavailable, use plywood of the same thickness.*

INSTRUCTIONS

1. Enlarge the cutting patterns. Then transfer the body shape onto 3/4"-thick stock and the mouth sides, tail, and legs onto 1/4"-thick stock. Also transfer the hole locations.

2. Cut out the wooden shapes, using your jigsaw and scrolling blade. (Don't make the curved interior mouth cut yet.)

3. Apply a little glue to the inside faces of the mouth sides and clamp them onto either side of the body so that the edges align neatly. Then glue and clamp the paired front and rear leg pieces onto the body as well. Let the assembly dry thoroughly.

4. After removing the clamps from the assembly, use your jigsaw to create the mouth.

5. Through the body, bore the two 7/16" axles holes. Then, in the edge of the body, bore the 1/2" hole, 1-5/8" deep, for the push stick.

6. Bore the 1/8" hole through the tail. Centered across the bottom edge of the body, 1-1/8" from the pointed end, bore the 1/16" pilot hole, 3/4" deep, for the screw that will attach the tail.

7. Using your backsaw and miter box, cut the four axles and the push stick to length. Round the axle ends with your flat rasp.

8. With your compass, draw four 3-3/8"-diameter circles on 3/4" stock; cut them out carefully with your jigsaw.

9. Locate the wheel centers with your center finder, mark them with your pencil, and bore a 3/8" through-hole at each mark.

10. In each wheel, locate and mark the cut that will hold the rubber flipper. Make the cuts with your backsaw.

11. Lay out the push-stick handle on a scrap of 1-1/2"-thick stock and cut it to size with your circular saw. Use extra caution when cutting this small part!

12. Bore the 1/2" hole, 1" deep, in the center of one end of the handle.

13. Rasp and sand all parts thoroughly and remove the sanding debris.

14. Prime the wooden parts with a quality primer. Then, as an undercoat, apply a couple of coats of gloss-brown latex enamel paint. Use gloss black and gloss red to detail the hair and eyes.

15. Lay out two flipper patterns on the smoothest side of the stair-tread material. Then turn the pattern over and lay out two more flippers. Cut out the shapes with your utility knife, trimming all edges neatly.

16. Bore two 3/64" pilot holes, 1-1/4" deep, adjacent to each wheel's saw cut (see the detail of the wheel). Install the flippers in the cuts; if the stair-tread material doesn't slip in easily, enlarge the cuts with sandpaper. Then pin each flipper in place by driving two 4d finishing nails into the holes.

17. Slip a wheel onto an axle, allowing 1/4" to project from the wheel's outside face. Slide a 3/8" cut washer over the axle's long end and push this end through either 7/16" hole in the body. (The flipper should point towards the creature's mouth.) Install a washer and wheel on the other end of the axle, this time turning the flipper towards the creature's rear end. The two flippers should be positioned exactly 180 degrees from each other.

18. Install the second wheels-and-axle set in the other 7/16" hole. Secure the wheels to the axles with 6d nails (see page 39).

19. Slip a 3/16" washer over a 1-1/4" deck screw and slide the screw through the 1/8" hole in the tail. Place another cut washer over the screw and insert the screw tip into the 1/16" pilot hole in the body, tightening it just enough so that the tail flops back and forth without resistance. (Position the "pointer" on the tail between the rear wheels.)

20. Using a bit of glue in each hole, install the push stick in the 1/2" holes in the body and push-stick handle.

21. With a bit of paint, touch up any problem areas created during wheel assembly. When the paint has dried, round up your kids and show them how Plato flaps his way along the floor. The best play surfaces for this project are slightly rough ones such as carpeting; hardwood flooring and vinyl floor coverings usually don't provide enough traction to spin Plato's wheels. Have fun!

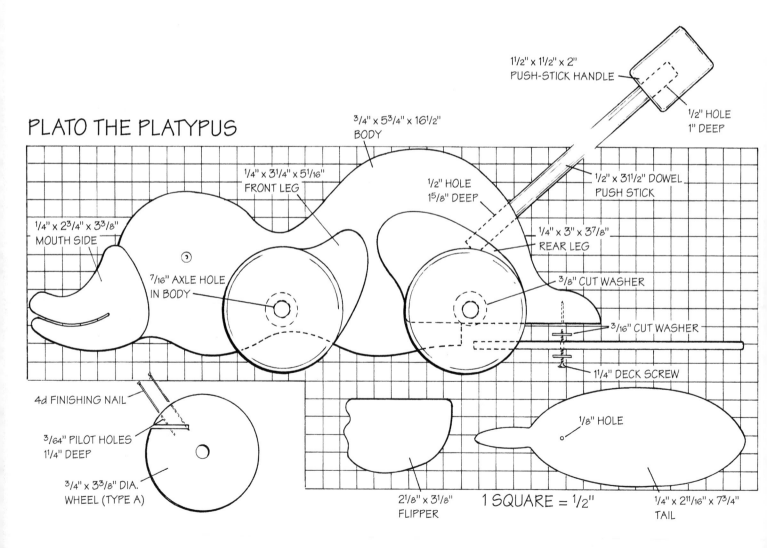

PLATO THE PLATYPUS

1½" x 1½" x 2"
PUSH-STICK HANDLE

½" HOLE
1" DEEP

¾" x 5³/4" x 16½"
BODY

¼" x 3¼" x 5¹/16"
FRONT LEG

½" HOLE
1⁵/8" DEEP

½" x 31½" DOWEL
PUSH STICK

¼" x 2³/4" x 3³/8"
MOUTH SIDE

7/16" AXLE HOLE
IN BODY

¼" x 3" x 3⁷/8"
REAR LEG

³/8" CUT WASHER

³/16" CUT WASHER

4d FINISHING NAIL

³/64" PILOT HOLES
1¼" DEEP

¾" x 3³/8" DIA.
WHEEL (TYPE A)

1¼" DECK SCREW

1/8" HOLE

2¹/8" x 3¹/8"
FLIPPER

1 SQUARE = ½"

¼" x 2¹¹/16" x 7³/4"
TAIL

**Rock and Roll!
Large Riding and Rolling Toys**

MINICYCLE

•••••

This little mover is hot, hot, hot!

TIPS

- *Use hardwood plywood for this project.*
- *Your plywood blade should have a minimum working length of at least 1-1/2".*
- *To assemble this project, you'll need approximately fifteen clamps with minimum jaw openings of 1-5/8".*

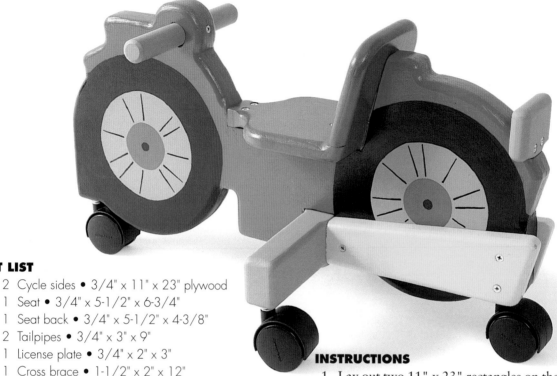

CUT LIST

2 Cycle sides • 3/4" x 11" x 23" plywood
1 Seat • 3/4" x 5-1/2" x 6-3/4"
1 Seat back • 3/4" x 5-1/2" x 4-3/8"
2 Tailpipes • 3/4" x 3" x 9"
1 License plate • 3/4" x 2" x 3"
1 Cross brace • 1-1/2" x 2" x 12"
1 Handle • 1" x 8" dowel

HARDWARE AND SUPPLIES

19 1-1/4" deck screws
4 2-1/2" deck screws
4 2" twin-wheel, stem-type, 75-lb. load rating swivel casters

SUGGESTED TOOLS

Layout tools
Backsaw and miter box
Circular saw
Jigsaw with medium-toothed and plywood blades
Paring chisel
Rasps
Claw hammer
No. 2 Phillips screwdriver
3/8" drill
1" bradpoint bit
Pilot bits for 1-1/4" and 2-1/2" deck screws
Bit sized to bore caster-mounting holes
Router with 3/8" rounding-over bit
Pad sander

INSTRUCTIONS

1. Lay out two 11" x 23" rectangles on the face of each 3/4" plywood piece.

2. Cut out the two rectangles with your circular saw and plywood blade. Glue and clamp the two rectangles together face to face, spacing the clamps approximately 2-1/2" apart throughout the rectangular shape. Let the glue dry.

3. Enlarge the cutting patterns for the cycle side, tailpipes, seat, and seat back. After removing the clamps from the glued plywood, transfer the cycle-side cutting pattern (and hole locations) to one side of the plywood assembly.

4. Cut out the cycle-side assembly with your jigsaw and plywood blade. Use a paring chisel to clean up the inside corners and flatten any irregular edges with your flat rasp.

5. Transfer the cutting patterns for the tailpipes, seat, and seat back, along with all hole locations, to the appropriate stock. Cut these parts to size, noting that the 5-1/2" edges of the seat and seat back are bevel-cut at 15-degree angles. Also cut the license plate and cross brace to size.

MINICYCLE

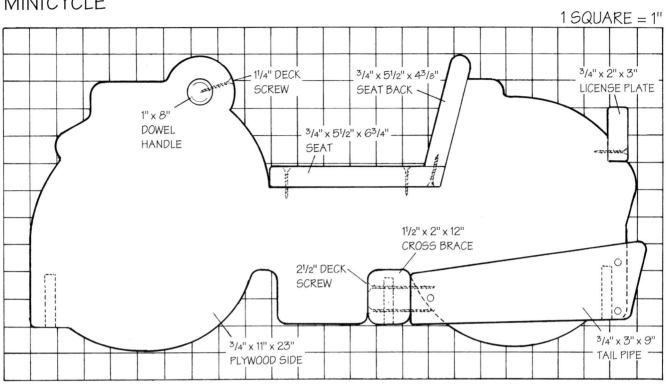

1¼" DECK SCREW

1" x 8" DOWEL HANDLE

¾" x 5½" x 4³/8" SEAT BACK

¾" x 5½" x 6¾" SEAT

¾" x 2" x 3" LICENSE PLATE

1½" x 2" x 12" CROSS BRACE

2½" DECK SCREW

¾" x 11" x 23" PLYWOOD SIDE

¾" x 3" x 9" TAIL PIPE

COMPONENT LAYOUT

1 SQUARE = 1"

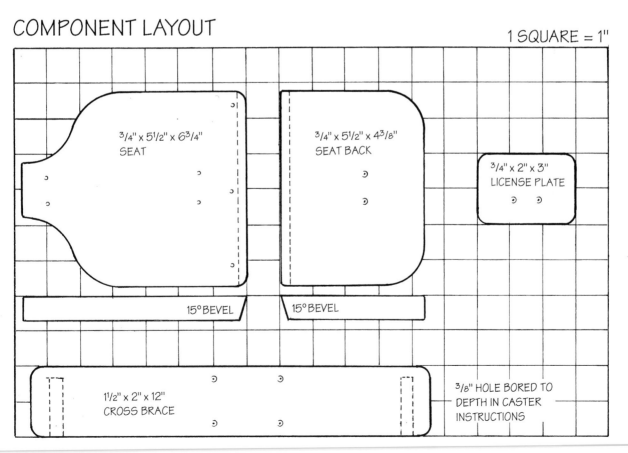

¾" x 5½" x 6¾" SEAT

¾" x 5½" x 4³/8" SEAT BACK

¾" x 2" x 3" LICENSE PLATE

15° BEVEL

15° BEVEL

1½" x 2" x 12" CROSS BRACE

³/8" HOLE BORED TO DEPTH IN CASTER INSTRUCTIONS

6. Using a router and 3/8" rounding-over bit, ease the arrises on all flat parts, taking care to avoid rounding those that will meet other arrises after the project is assembled. To soften the ends of the handle, use a flat rasp.

7. Bore the 1" handle hole in the cycle-side assembly.

8. Center the handle in the hole and, in the edge of the cycle-side assembly, bore the pilot hole for the 1-1/4" deck screw; the bit should pierce the handle. Remove the handle from the hole.

9. Test-fit all wooden parts, adjusting their sizes as necessary.

10. Bore the 3/8" caster-socket holes to the depth specified in the caster instructions, two in the bottom edge of the cross brace (see diagram of cross brace) and two in the bottom edge of the cycle-side assembly (see cycle-side cutting pattern).

11. Bore the remaining pilot holes for 1-1/4" deck screws as follows: three in each tailpipe; two in the license plate; two in the seat back; four in the seat's upper face; and three in the seat's bottom face, locating these last three at 15-degree angles to match the angle of the seat back. Also bore the four pilot holes for 2-1/2" deck screws in the cross brace.

12. Sand all parts thoroughly. (Some areas may need to be shaped with rasps before sanding.)

13. Fasten the seat pieces together with three 1-1/4" deck screws driven through the bottom face of the seat. Then install the seat assembly in the angled cutout on the cycle-side assembly and fasten it in place with four 1-1/4" deck screws driven through the seat and two driven through the seat back. Also install the license plate with two 1-1/4" deck screws.

14. Fasten one face of the cross brace to the square ends of the tailpipes, using four 2-1/2" deck screws. Then, using three 1-1/4" deck screws driven through the face of each tailpipe, fasten the assembled pieces to the bottom edge of the cycle-side assembly.

15. Reinsert the handle and fasten it with a 1-1/4" deck screw (see Step 8).

16. Install the casters, following the manufacturer's directions.

17. After wiping all sanding dust from the Minicycle, prime and paint the project with latex finishes. The wheel and fender details shown in the photo were marked and painted after priming.

hilarious hill racers

A No. 2 washtub, some wheels, working brakes, and a lot of nerve are the key ingredients in the Chimney Rock Hillfall, held high in the mountains of Chimney Rock Park, North Carolina. This fanciful, gravity-powered racing event was started in the 1970s by one Rick Gambill, who imagined the lowly metal washtub as required equipment for every racer. What started as a joke has since evolved into a well-attended event that tickles the public's funny bone once a year.

The races—both competition and exhibition matches—are overseen by the Gravity Tub Racer's Association. The competition tub racers are towed uphill to the starting line at an elevation of nearly 2000 feet (607 m), where they prepare their wacky vehicles for take-off and then depart in pairs. Reaching speeds of 60 MPH (96.5 km/h), the racers scream through hairpin turns as they drop 525 vertical feet (160 m) towards the finish line below.

Exhibition tubbers are less concerned with speed than they are with making a lasting impression on the spectators. Memorable entries have included a NASA spaceship and a stagecoach.

While Association rules ensure a safe event for drivers and spectators alike, they don't influence the tub racers' designs, which are limited only by their builders' imaginations and the availability of scrap parts for creative decoration.

When the race day is over, the lucky winners take home their coveted washboard trophies, and runners-up stow their contraptions and nurse their pride. Next year the gravity tubbers will be back on the mountain again, ready to roll!

The "bumble-bee" tub. Courtesy of Chimney Rock Park, North Carolina.

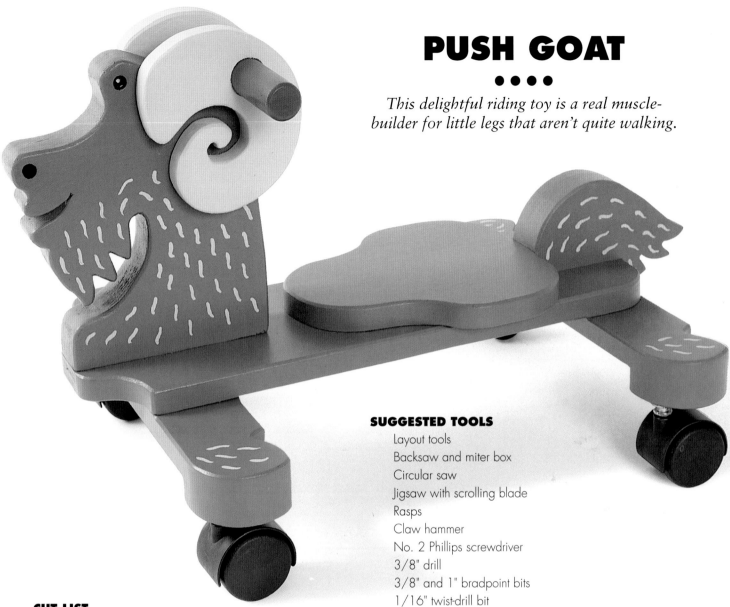

PUSH GOAT

• • • •

This delightful riding toy is a real muscle-builder for little legs that aren't quite walking.

CUT LIST

1   Base • 3/4" x 5-1/2" x 18"
2   Legs • 3/4" x 2-1/2" x 14"
4   Caster supports • 3/4" x 2" x 2-1/2"
1   Seat • 3/4" x 7-1/4" x 8"
1   Tail • 1-1/2" x 3-3/8" x 5-5/8"
1   Head • 1-1/2" x 7-1/2" x 8-7/16"
2   Horns • 3/4" x 4-3/4" x 5"
1   Handle • 1" x 8" dowel

HARDWARE AND SUPPLIES

13   1-1/4" deck screws
6   2" deck screws
2   3d finishing nails
4   2" twin-wheel, stem-type, 75-lb. load rating swivel casters

SUGGESTED TOOLS

Layout tools
Backsaw and miter box
Circular saw
Jigsaw with scrolling blade
Rasps
Claw hammer
No. 2 Phillips screwdriver
3/8" drill
3/8" and 1" bradpoint bits
1/16" twist-drill bit
Bit sized to bore caster-mounting holes
Pilot bits for 1-1/4", 1-5/8", and 2" deck screws
Router with chamfer bit adjusted for 1/8" cut
Pad sander

TIPS

- *For a clean look, recess the screws and nails in the horns. Fill the holes and sand them flat before painting.*

- *A hardware store or industrial supplier can provide you with the casters. Check the depth of the stem bore-hole listed on the caster package; if the depth is greater than 1-3/8", cut the four caster support pieces from stock that's at least 1". Regardless of the stock's thickness, instructions are identical for cutting, boring, and assembling these pieces.*

INSTRUCTIONS

1. Enlarge all the cutting patterns and transfer them (including all hole locations) to stock of appropriate thickness.

2. Carefully cut all the parts to size, using your circular saw, your jigsaw with scrolling blade, and—for the handle—your backsaw and miter box. Note that the shapes of the caster supports are identical to those of the ends of the legs.

3. Carefully smooth all saw cuts, using your rasp and sandpaper and paying particular attention to deep cuts such as those in the mouth and tail.

4. Apply a little glue to the upper faces of the caster supports. Then clamp the supports onto the ends of the legs, aligning the edges carefully.

5. Bore the eyes and nostrils on both sides of the head, using a 3/8" bradpoint bit and a collar adjusted for a 1/4" depth. Then, though the horns, bore the holes for the handles, using a 1" bradpoint bit.

6. Bore the 3/8" caster-stem holes (according to the manufacturer's instructions) in the bottoms of the caster supports.

7. Using the diagram as a guide, bore the pilot holes for 1-1/4" and 2" deck screws in the horns, legs, and base as follows:

   • Two holes for 2" screws in the bottom of the rear leg, to fasten the rear leg and tail to the base
   • Four holes for 2" screws in the bottom of the base, to fasten the head
   • Two holes for 1-1/4" screws in the top of the base, to secure the rear leg

PUSH GOAT

1 SQUARE = 1"

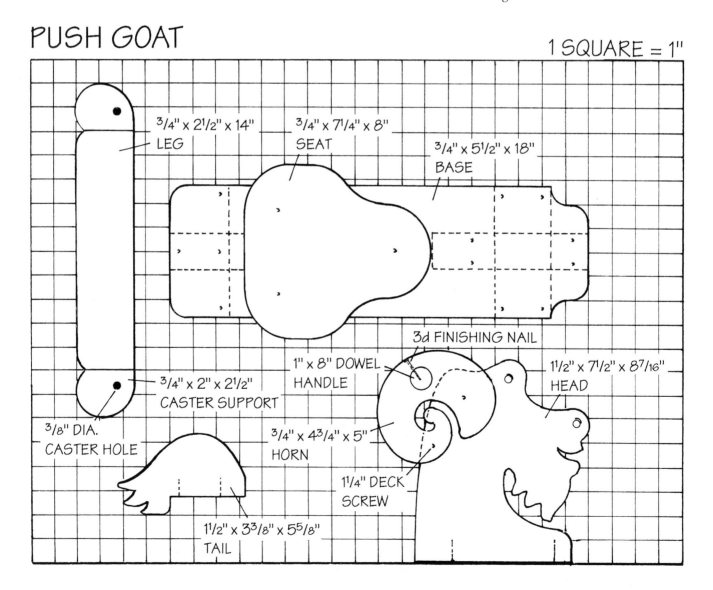

3/4" x 2 1/2" x 14"
LEG

3/4" x 7 1/4" x 8"
SEAT

3/4" x 5 1/2" x 18"
BASE

3d FINISHING NAIL

1" x 8" DOWEL
HANDLE

1 1/2" x 7 1/2" x 8 7/16"
HEAD

3/4" x 2" x 2 1/2"
CASTER SUPPORT

3/8" DIA.
CASTER HOLE

3/4" x 4 3/4" x 5"
HORN

1 1/4" DECK
SCREW

1 1/2" x 3 3/8" x 5 5/8"
TAIL

- Four holes for 1-1/4" screws in the top of the base, to secure the front leg
- Three holes for 1-1/4" screws in the bottom of the base, to fasten the seat
- Two holes for 1-1/4" screws in each horn, to secure the horns to the head

8. Clamp the base, legs, tail, and seat together temporarily and mark the locations where the arrises will need routing to make them comfortable for little fingers. Disassemble the parts and chamfer the marked arrises, using your router fitted with a chamfer bit adjusted for a 1/8" cut.

9. Repeat Step 8, this time dry-clamping the head-and-horns assembly before marking, disassembling, and routing these parts. Ease tight corners that the router bit can't reach—such as those in the beard, mouth, and tail—with a flat rasp and sandpaper.

10. Sand all parts well.

11. To assemble the Push Goat, first fasten the back leg to the bottom surface of the base and the tail to the top surface, positioning both pieces perpendicular to the length of the base, with the hooves pointing backwards and the edge of the back leg flush with the base's end.

12. Position the front leg with its front edge 1-5/8" from the front end of the base and fasten it in place with four 1-1/4" deck screws.

13. Secure the seat next, butting its back edge against the front edge of the tail, centering its length across the width of the base, and fastening the piece in place with three 1-1/4" deck screws driven through the base.

14. Align the head so that the front edge of the neck is flush with the front edge of the base and fasten it with four 2" deck screws driven through the base.

15. Secure the horns to the head with 1-1/4" deck screws. Then bore a 1/16" pilot hole into the upper edge of each horn, aiming the bit toward the handle hole. Fasten the handle in its matching holes by driving 3d finishing nails into these pilot holes.

16. Before installing the casters in their mounting holes, finish the project in any way that appeals to you. The project in the photograph was painted with latex enamel paints and two coats of water-based varnish to provide a "kid-proof" finish. Then press the casters and their sockets in place and you're done!

TRUNDLE BLOCK WAGON

•••••

*Children learning to walk will love this
little block wagon built just for them.*

CUT LIST

2 Sides • 3/4" x 3-1/2" x 16"
2 Front and back • 3/4" x 3-1/2" x 10-3/4"
1 Bottom • 1/2" x 6-5/8" x 10-3/4" plywood
2 Handle supports • 3/4" x 7-1/4" x 17"
3 Handles • 1" x 14-1/4" dowel
4 Axles • 3/4" x 1-3/4" dowel
4 Wheels • 3/4" x 4"-diameter
4 Axle pins • 1/4" x 1-1/4" dowel
7 Blocks • 1-1/2" x 1-1/2" x 6-3/8"
2 Long supports • 3/4" x 3/4" x 10-11/16"
2 Short supports • 3/4" x 3/4" x 5-1/16"

HARDWARE AND SUPPLIES

8 1-5/8" deck screws
20 1-1/4" deck screws
20 No. 18 x 1" brads
6 6d finishing nails

SUGGESTED TOOLS

Layout tools
Backsaw and miter box
Circular saw
Jigsaw with scrolling blade
Claw hammer
No. 2 Phillips screwdriver
3/8" drill
1/4", 3/4", 13/16", and 1" bradpoint bits
1/16" twist-drill bit
Pilot bits for 1-1/4" and 1-5/8" deck screws
Router with chamfer bit adjusted for 3/16" cut
Pad sander

INSTRUCTIONS

1. Lay out all 3/4"-thick parts and cut them to rough length. Also cut to length the eleven dowel parts and the blocks. Finally, lay out and cut the plywood bottom piece to size.

2. Using your compass, lay out a 1-3/4" radius half-circle at each end of each side piece. Cut the marked radii with your jigsaw and scrolling blade.

3. On the outer face of each side piece, mark four pilot-hole locations for 1-5/8" deck screws. Locate one pair 2-1/4" from one end of each piece and the other pair 6-3/8" from the opposite end of each piece; all four holes are 3/8" from the edges. Bore the holes with a pilot bit for 1-5/8" deck screws.

4. Set the two side pieces on your work surface with the pilot-hole counterbores facing up and the sets of holes in the pieces arranged in opposite directions from one another. (The pieces should be stretched left to right in front of you.) Locate and bore a pair of 3/4" axle holes, 1/2" deep, in each side piece; the holes should be 2-1/4" from each end and 1-3/8" from the edge nearest you. (These edges will be the bottom edges when the wagon is assembled.)

5. Flip the side pieces over, and centered over the back of each 3/4" axle hole, mark and bore a pilot hole for a 1-1/4" deck screw.

6. To lay out the handle supports on the rough lengths of 3/4" stock that you cut, first cut each piece to a truncated right-triangle shape, 3-5/16" wide at one end and 7-1/4" wide at the other. At the narrow end of each piece, mark a 1-7/8" radius half-circle. Then cut these radii with your jigsaw. Lay out a 2-1/8" radius semicircle near the right-angle corner of each piece, locating its center on the longest arris, 1-3/8" from the right-angled corner. After sawing out the two semicircles, cut off the sharply-pointed corner from the bottom of each side piece, to create a 1/2"-long flat on each one. (These will help to keep little fingers safe.)

7. In opposing faces of the two handle supports, lay out four pilot holes for 1-1/4" deck screws and three 1" handle through-holes as follows:
   • Two pilot holes, 3/4" from the bottom end and 1" and 2-3/4" from the angled front edge
   • Two pilot holes, 2-3/4" from the bottom end and 2-3/4" and 4-1/2" from the angled front edge
   • Three handle holes, 1-7/8" from the back edge and 7-1/4", 11-1/4", and 15-1/4" from the bottom end

8. Bore the marked pilot holes and handle through-holes in each handle support. Remember to lay out and bore the pieces in mirror-image fashion as the pieces will be mounted opposite to one another.

9. Through one face of each long and short support piece, bore pilot holes for 1-1/4" deck screws, spacing four holes equally in each long support and two holes equally in each short support.

10. Lay out and cut the four wheels to size. Then mark and carefully bore a 13/16" through-hole in the center of each wheel, using a center finder for accurate layout.

11. Secure a dowel axle and mark a point 1/2" from an end. Bore a 1/4" through-hole at that point. Repeat with the other three axles.

12. Thoroughly sand all parts, carefully easing all arrises on the blocks and any arrises that will be exposed when your project is assembled. The exposed arrises on our wagon were eased with a router fitted with a chamfer bit adjusted for a 3/16" cut. The chamfer locations were marked while the project pieces were temporarily clamped together; the pieces were then chamfered individually.

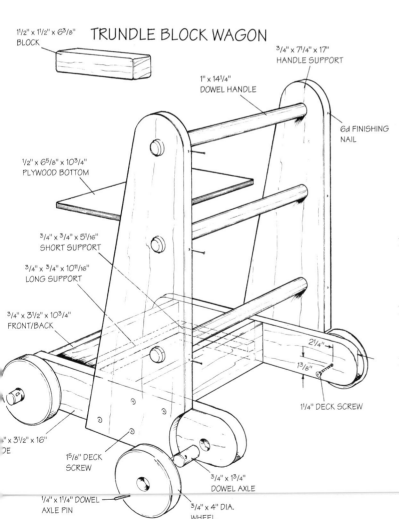

TRUNDLE BLOCK WAGON

1½" x 1½" x 6³⁄₈" BLOCK

3/4" x 7¼" x 17" HANDLE SUPPORT

1" x 14¼" DOWEL HANDLE

6d FINISHING NAIL

½" x 6⅝" x 10³⁄₄" PLYWOOD BOTTOM

¾" x ¾" x 5¹⁄₁₆" SHORT SUPPORT

¾" x ¾" x 10¹¹⁄₁₆" LONG SUPPORT

¾" x 3½" x 10³⁄₄" FRONT/BACK

2¼"

1³⁄₈"

1¼" DECK SCREW

¾" x 3½" x 16" SIDE

1⁵⁄₈" DECK SCREW

¾" x 13¾" DOWEL AXLE

¼" x 1¼" DOWEL AXLE PIN

¾" x 4" DIA. WHEEL

13. To prevent the axles from splitting when screws are inserted into them, bore a 1/16" pilot hole, 1" deep, in the center of one end of each axle. Then install the bored ends of the axles in their respective side pieces' holes, applying a few drops of glue at each joint and orienting the axle-pin holes identically with one another. Secure the axles with 1-1/4" deck screws driven through the pilot holes bored in Step 5.

14. Fasten the front and back pieces inside of the side pieces and secure them with 1-5/8" deck screws. The front piece's front face aligns 1-7/8" from the front ends of the side pieces; the back piece's front face aligns 9-1/4" from the same point.

15. Slip the wheels in place and install the axle pins, adjusting them so that they protrude evenly from each side of the pin holes and applying a drop of glue with each one.

16. Install the four supports inside the box assembly so that their bottom edges are 1-1/4" from the bottom edges of the sides, front piece, and back piece.

17. Fasten the bottom piece onto the supports with 1" brads spaced equally around the bottom piece's face; use a brad setter to seat the brads in the supports.

18. Attach the two handle supports by inserting 1-1/4" deck screws into the pilot holes bored in Step 7, allowing approximately 1/8" clearance between the semicircular cutouts and the rear wheels.

19. Finish the blocks and the handles in bright latex paint colors, applying several coats.

20. Slide the handles through the paired holes in the handle supports, allowing the ends of each one to extend equally from the handle supports' outside faces.

21. Bore 1/16" holes, 1-3/4" deep, each centered in the back edge of a handle support directly over each handle; the bit should pierce the handle. Then drive 6d finishing nails into the holes to secure the handles.

22. Give the Trundle Block Wagon and blocks a couple of coats of water-based varnish and you're all set!

the woodcarvers of Sonepur, India

Wheeled toys are handcrafted around the world. In Sonepur, India, four families of woodworkers display their carved toys during the festival of Lanka Podi, which commemorates a story from the *Ramayana*, an ancient Hindu epic poem. In this story, the heroic monkey-general, Hanuman, comes to Lanka, the golden fortress of the demon leader, Ravana, in search of the kidnapped heroine, Sita. Ravana traps Hanuman and sets his tail on fire. Hanuman, however, turns the tables on Ravana by using his blazing tail to set Lanka on fire.

Carved and brightly painted, the elaborately detailed toys brought out at this festival include elephants (complete with riders) and emblems of prosperity such as the Wishing Cow, said to grant wishes to anyone who touches it.

If you look closely at the photo above, you'll see that the wheel-and-axle construction of the toys depicted is a variant of the method used with the Trundle Block Wagon in this book. Some techniques just can't be improved upon!

Wood toys made by Hadu Maharana, Sonepur (western Orissa), India, 1993.

Courtesy of Joanna Williams (photographer) and the San Francisco Craft & Folk Art Musem.

RATTLE MOWER

••••

The gentle click-clack of this mower's
rattle mechanism makes cutting
the grass child's play.

CUT LIST

2 Long braces • 3/4" x 1-1/2" x 24"
1 Short brace • 3/4" x 2-1/2" x 10-1/2"
2 Handle and axle • 3/4" x 12-1/4" dowel
2 Wheels • 3/4" x 7-1/4"-diameter
6 Stretchers • 7/16" x 9-1/2" dowel
8 Rattles • 1" x 3-3/4" dowel
16 Pins • 1/8" x 5/8" dowel

HARDWARE AND SUPPLIES

4 1-5/8" deck screws
4 3d finishing nails

SUGGESTED TOOLS

Layout tools
Backsaw and miter box
Circular saw
Coping saw
Jigsaw with medium-toothed and scrolling blades
Claw hammer
3/8" drill
7/16", 1/2", 3/4", and 13/16" bradpoint bits
1/8" twist-drill bit
Router with chamfer bit adjusted
    for 3/16" cut
Pad sander

TIP

• *For a clear picture of how this project is assembled,*
  take an occasional look at the photo as you work.

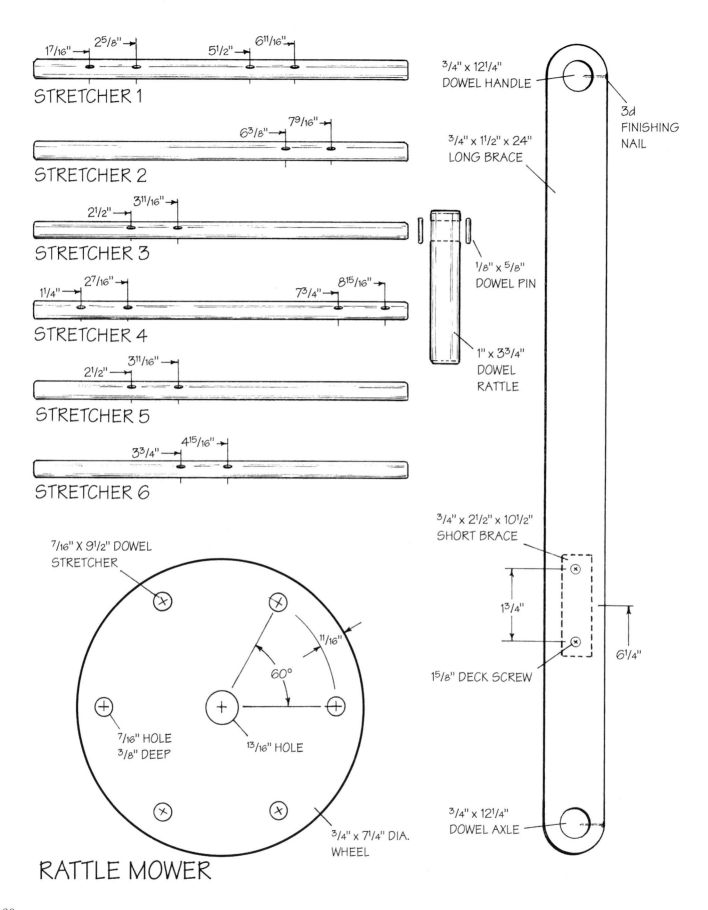

$1^7/_{16}$" $2^5/_8$" $5^1/_2$" $6^{11}/_{16}$"

STRETCHER 1

$6^3/_8$" $7^9/_{16}$"

STRETCHER 2

$2^1/_2$" $3^{11}/_{16}$"

STRETCHER 3

$1^1/_4$" $2^7/_{16}$" $7^3/_4$" $8^{15}/_{16}$"

STRETCHER 4

$2^1/_2$" $3^{11}/_{16}$"

STRETCHER 5

$3^3/_4$" $4^{15}/_{16}$"

STRETCHER 6

$3/_4$" x $12^1/_4$"
DOWEL HANDLE

3d
FINISHING
NAIL

$3/_4$" x $1^1/_2$" x 24"
LONG BRACE

$1/_8$" x $5/_8$"
DOWEL PIN

1" x $3^3/_4$"
DOWEL
RATTLE

$3/_4$" x $2^1/_2$" x $10^1/_2$"
SHORT BRACE

$1^3/_4$"

$6^1/_4$"

$1^5/_8$" DECK SCREW

$3/_4$" x $12^1/_4$"
DOWEL AXLE

$7/_{16}$" X $9^1/_2$" DOWEL
STRETCHER

$11/_{16}$"

$60°$

$7/_{16}$" HOLE
$3/_8$" DEEP

$13/_{16}$" HOLE

$3/_4$" x $7^1/_4$" DIA.
WHEEL

RATTLE MOWER

INSTRUCTIONS

1. Lay out and cut to length both the long braces and the short brace.

2. Using your compass, mark 3/4" radii on the ends of the long braces. Cut the marked radii with your jigsaw and scrolling blade.

3. Locate a mark 3/4" from each end of each long brace, centering it across the face, and bore a 3/4" through-hole at each mark. The handle will fit into the hole at one end, and the axle will fit into the other.

4. With your compass, lay out two 7-1/4"-diameter wheels on the face of a piece of 3/4" stock. Cut the wheels out with your jigsaw and medium-toothed blade.

5. To lay out locations for the stretchers that run between the two wheels, first use your center finder to locate the center of each wheel; then mark these centers. Divide each wheel into six equal "pie shapes" by drawing diameter lines through the marked center.

6. Locate and mark a point 11/16" from each line's outer end. Then bore a 7/16" hole, 3/8" deep, at each point.

7. Complete the wheels by boring a 13/16" hole through each wheel's center mark.

8. Using your backsaw and miter box, cut the six 7/16" dowel stretchers to 9-1/2" lengths.

9. To receive the paired pins that secure the rattles in place, each stretcher must be bored through its thickness with a 1/8" bit (see the stretchers in the diagram). The holes in each pair of holes are 1-3/16" apart and are bored in the same direction. Four stretchers have one pair of pin holes each; two stretchers have two pairs of pin holes each. Start by labeling the stretchers 1 through 6. Then, aligning the stretchers on your work surface and measuring from the same end of each one, mark the stretchers as shown in the diagram.

10. Carefully bore a 1/8" through-hole at each mark.

11. Using your utility knife or coping saw, cut the sixteen 1/8" dowel pins to 5/8" lengths.

12. Saw the eight dowel rattles to 3-3/4" lengths.

13. In each rattle, a 1/2" through-hole must be bored so that the rattles can be slipped onto the stretchers. To simplify this process and to avoid tear-out at the exit point of the drill bit, make a simple jig to support the rattles (see Boring Jig diagram). First, bore a 1"-diameter through-hole in a 1-1/2" thick scrap board, locating the hole's center 1" from the board's end. Slide a dowel rattle into the hole so that a 1/4"-deep space remains at the end of the rattle inside of the

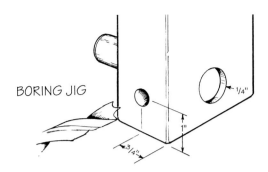

BORING JIG

hole. Now, mark the edge of the board for boring so that your 1/2" bit will bore a hole that is centered in the dowel rattle's thickness, 1/2" from its end. Use this jig to bore all the rattles.

14. Sand all parts well. Using a router fitted with a 3/16" chamfer bit, chamfer the arrises of the braces and wheels. (Avoid chamfering the ends of the short brace.)

15. Install the rattles on the stretchers. Then insert and glue the pins in place around each one. Avoid gluing the rattles!

16. Glue the stretchers' ends into the 7/16" holes of one wheel, making sure to arrange them around the wheel's circumference in their numerical order. Then glue the other wheel onto the stretchers' other ends. Locate the free ends of the rattles inside the cage created by the stretchers and wheels.

17. Assemble the braces, centering the ends of the short brace 6-1/4" from the ends of the long braces; center these ends across the long braces' widths as well. Secure the short brace by driving a pair of pilot-bored 1-5/8" deck screws, 1-3/4" apart, through each long brace and into each end of the short brace.

18. Install the handle in the 3/4" through-holes farthest from the short brace so that it projects 1/8" beyond the outside face of each brace. Bore a 1/32" pilot hole in each long brace, 3/4" deep, 3/4" from the end closest to the handle, and centered across each edge; the drill bit should pierce the dowel handle. Secure the handle with two 3d finishing nails driven into these predrilled holes.

19. Complete the mower by sliding the axle through the long braces' remaining holes and through the wheeled assembly, securing the axle as in Step 18. Note that the clacking sounds should be made by the rattles striking the axle rather than each other, so do locate the dowels accordingly before securing the axle in place. Finish the mower with several coats of a transparent or colored finish, following the manufacturer's directions.

TUGGY BOAT

● ● ● ●

Arrrrrrr! Young mariners won't be able to resist this rolling boat with its twin portholes, working storage hatch, and anchor. To build the matching Barge project, turn to page 87.

CUT LIST

- 2 Hull sides • 3/4" x 12" x 30" plywood
- 2 Cabin sides • 3/4" x 10" x 20" plywood
- 2 Cabin trims • 3/4" x 2-1/2" x 12-1/2" plywood
- 1 Cabin back • 3/4" x 16" x 18" plywood
- 1 Seat • 3/4" x 9-7/8" x 16" plywood
- 1 Hatch bottom • 3/4" x 7-1/2" x 16" plywood
- 1 Hatch back • 3/4" x 4" x 16" plywood
- 1 Hatch cover • 3/4" x 8-1/2" x 15-3/4" plywood
- 1 Anchor • 3/4" x 5" x 6" plywood
- 2 Hatch-cover supports • 3/4" x 3-1/4" x 4-1/2"
- 2 Porthole trims • 3/4" x 5"-diameter
- 1 Anchor-line hole trim • 3/4" x 3"-diameter
- 1 Handle • 1" x 18-1/2" dowel
- 1 Flagpole • 1" x 26" dowel
- 2 Hatch-cover pins • 3/8" x 2" dowel
- 1 Rear caster support • 3/4" x 1-1/2" x 16"
- 2 Front caster supports • 1-1/2" x 3" x 12"

HARDWARE AND SUPPLIES

- 1 lb. 1-1/4" deck screws
- 3 1-5/8" deck screws
- 2 2-5/8" deck screws
- 4 2" twin-wheel, stem-type, 75-lb. load rating casters
- 2 Size 112 small screw eyes
- 2 3/8" cut washers
- 1 48" length of 1/8" nylon rope
- 1 6' length of 3/4" nylon rope
- 1 6" x 6-1/2" piece nylon "ripstop" fabric
-    Thread to match fabric color
-    Plastic tape

SUGGESTED TOOLS

- Layout tools
- Backsaw and miter box
- Circular saw
- Jigsaw with plywood and scrolling blades
- Rasps
- Claw hammer
- 3/8" drill
- 1/16" twist-drill bit
- 3/8" and 13/32" bradpoint bits
- Pilot bits for 1-1/4" and 1-5/8" deck screws
- Router with 3/8" rounding-over bit
- Pad sander
- Needle

TIPS

- *The relative complexity of this project makes it a good choice for more experienced builders.*

- *Use hardwood plywood for the main parts and hardwoods for the solid wood parts. For outdoor use, substitute pressure-treated plywood and lumber and use exterior-grade finishes.*

- *Before making and installing the front and rear caster supports, temporarily clamp together the plywood parts and check to see that the casters you purchased will extend below the project's bottom edges by at least 3/4" when installed. The casters shouldn't touch the inner faces of the hull sides when they rotate in their sockets. Adjust the height and location of the supports as required; their height can also be raised to accommodate the longer legs of taller children.*

- *For Step 9, you'll need several C-clamps and four clamps with minimum jaw openings of 17-5/8".*

INSTRUCTIONS

1. This project requires many layouts! Start by enlarging and transferring the cutting patterns for the hull sides and anchor (see pages 84 and 86), including all hole locations.

2. Through the outside face of each hull side, bore the pilot holes for 1-1/4" deck screws: one hole to enter the edge of the hatch back; three to enter the edge of the hatch bottom; and three to enter the edge of the seat. Also bore the 1-1/4"-diameter anchor-line hole (in one hull side only), the 1"-diameter handle holes, and the 3/8" holes for the hatch-cover pins (see diagram).

3. Here come the layouts! Study the photos and diagrams carefully before tackling this step; when hole locations are not provided in the diagrams, they're provided here. Lay out the remaining ten plywood parts and mark pilot-hole locations for 1-1/4" deck screws as follows:

   • Through the inside face of each cabin side, six holes to enter each hull side

   • Through the outside face of each cabin side, six holes to enter each edge of the cabin back

   • Through the outside face of each cabin trim, three holes to enter each cabin side

   • Through the hatch-side face of the cabin back, two holes to enter the ends of the front caster supports, each hole located 1-1/2" from the bottom edge and 2-1/8" in from an end; and five holes to enter the back edge of the seat, located 1", 4-1/2", 8", 11-1/2", and 15" from an end and 2-5/8" from the bottom edge

   • Through the seat-side face of the cabin back, five holes to enter the hatch bottom, located 1", 4-1/2", 8", 11-1/2", and 15" from an end, and 3/8" in from the bottom edge

   • Through the upper face of the seat, two rows of three holes to enter the front caster supports, located 1", 4-7/8", and 8" from each edge and 2-1/8" from each end

   • Through the outer face of the hatch back, five holes to enter the edge of the hatch bottom, located 3/8" from an edge and 1", 4-1/2", 8", 11-1/2", and 15" from an end

4. Referring to both the Cross Section and Front View diagrams, lay out the locations where the various plywood parts will fasten together. Strike lines with a straight edge where necessary to be certain all locations are clearly indicated.

5. Cut out all the plywood parts. Note that the cabin back is 16" wide at its base and 14-1/2" wide at its top end; a 3/4" x 15" cutout is made along each edge so that the remaining 14-1/2" width will fit between the cabin sides.

6. Bore all the marked deck-screw pilot holes and all other through-holes in the plywood parts. To start the porthole and anchor-line holes, first bore a 3/8" starting hole inside each layout; then make the cutouts with your jigsaw.

7. Lay out and cut to size the hatch-cover supports and the rear and front caster supports (see "Tips" before you begin this step). Mark these parts for routing, using the photos as a guide.

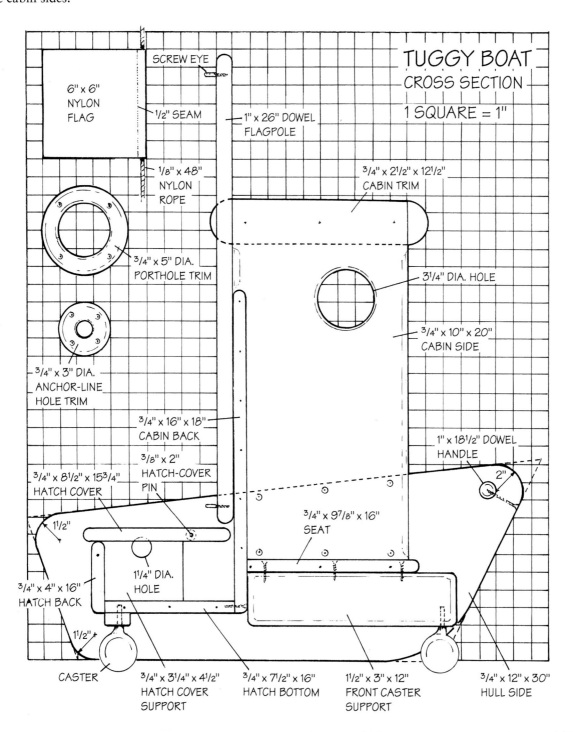

TUGGY BOAT
CROSS SECTION
1 SQUARE = 1"

6" x 6" NYLON FLAG

SCREW EYE

1/2" SEAM

1" x 26" DOWEL FLAGPOLE

1/8" x 48" NYLON ROPE

3/4" x 2 1/2" x 12 1/2" CABIN TRIM

3/4" x 5" DIA. PORTHOLE TRIM

3 1/4" DIA. HOLE

3/4" x 10" x 20" CABIN SIDE

3/4" x 3" DIA. ANCHOR-LINE HOLE TRIM

3/4" x 16" x 18" CABIN BACK

3/8" x 2" HATCH-COVER PIN

3/4" x 8 1/2" x 15 3/4" HATCH COVER

1" x 18 1/2" DOWEL HANDLE

2"

3/4" x 9 7/8" x 16" SEAT

1 1/2"

1 1/4" DIA. HOLE

3/4" x 4" x 16" HATCH BACK

1 1/2"

CASTER

3/4" x 3 1/4" x 4 1/2" HATCH COVER SUPPORT

3/4" x 7 1/2" x 16" HATCH BOTTOM

1 1/2" x 3" x 12" FRONT CASTER SUPPORT

3/4" x 12" x 30" HULL SIDE

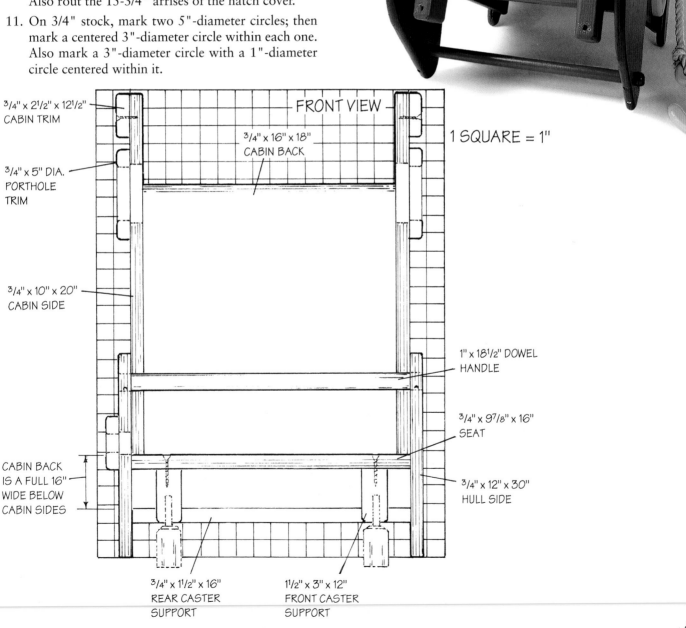

8. Mark and bore pilot holes for 1-1/4" deck screws in these support pieces as follows:
   • Through the rear caster support, five holes to enter the hatch bottom, centered along the 1-1/2" face, 3-1/2" apart
   • Through each hatch-cover support, four holes to enter each hull side, one hole in each corner, 3/4" from an edge and adjacent edge

9. Using the layouts that you made earlier, temporarily clamp all the plywood parts together except for the hatch cover. Then mark the locations for routing the 3/8" round-overs on all parts; avoid routing arrises that will meet each other once assembled.

10. Disassemble the parts and rout the round-overs. Also rout the 15-3/4" arrises of the hatch cover.

11. On 3/4" stock, mark two 5"-diameter circles; then mark a centered 3"-diameter circle within each one. Also mark a 3"-diameter circle with a 1"-diameter circle centered within it.

3/4" x 2¹/2" x 12¹/2" CABIN TRIM

FRONT VIEW

1 SQUARE = 1"

3/4" x 16" x 18" CABIN BACK

3/4" x 5" DIA. PORTHOLE TRIM

3/4" x 10" x 20" CABIN SIDE

1" x 18¹/2" DOWEL HANDLE

3/4" x 9⁷/8" x 16" SEAT

CABIN BACK IS A FULL 16" WIDE BELOW CABIN SIDES

3/4" x 12" x 30" HULL SIDE

3/4" x 1¹/2" x 16" REAR CASTER SUPPORT

1¹/2" x 3" x 12" FRONT CASTER SUPPORT

12. Before cutting the circular pieces out, mark and bore the four equidistant pilot holes for 1-1/4" deck screws in each layout.

13. Make the inner cutouts first. Bore starter holes as in Step 6 and make the cutouts with your jigsaw.

14. Using your router, round over the cutouts' arrises on both faces.

15. Cut the larger layouts to free the trim pieces from the stock.

16. Routing small parts such as these is dangerous unless the parts are well secured beforehand. One method is to firmly attach the parts to a fixed surface such as 3/4" plywood, using 1-1/4" screws driven from beneath the surface through pilot holes bored in the inner faces of each part. Make sure that the screw tips will remain well clear of the router bit and wear your safety glasses whenever you pick up your power tools.

17. Repeat Step 16 to rout the anchor's arrises.

18. Sand all parts thoroughly.

19. Clamp the various plywood parts together in proper alignment and fasten them with 1-1/4" deck screws driven through the pilot holes. (It's beginning to look a bit like a boat, isn't it?)

20. Using 1-1/4" deck screws, attach the porthole, anchor-line hole trims, and rear and front caster supports.

21. Mark and cut to length the hatch-cover pins, handle, and flagpole, and round both ends of each with a rasp.

22. Sand the dowel parts well.

23. In the flagpole, lay out and bore the three pilot holes for 1-5/8" deck screws, aligning them exactly along one edge.

24. Using three 1-5/8" deck screws, attach the flagpole to the anchor-hole side of the cabin back face; center the pole 3/4" from the edge of the hatch back, positioning it so that there will be a little clearance between the bottom of the pole and the upper face of the hatch cover.

25. Center the handle in the two handle holes in the hull sides. Secure it in place with two pilot-bored 2-5/8" deck screws driven through the front edges of the hull sides; aim the drill bit so that its tip pierces the handle.

26. Bore a 3/8" hole, 1" deep, in each end of the hatch cover, 2-5/8" from an edge (see diagram for hole location). The hatch-cover pins will be inserted in these holes.

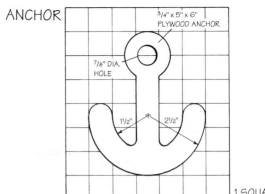

ANCHOR

3/4" x 5" x 6" PLYWOOD ANCHOR

7/8" DIA. HOLE

1 1/2"   2 1/2"

1 SQUARE = 1"

27. Place a drop or two of glue in each 3/8" hole in the hatch cover. Position the hatch cover between the hull sides, hold a cut washer in place between the inner face of one hull side and the end of the hatch cover, and insert a hatch-cover pin through the bored hole in the hull side. Repeat with the other cut washer and hatch-cover pin.

28. Using 1-1/4" deck screws, install the hatch-cover supports and the front and rear caster supports.

29. Bore the 3/8" caster-socket holes in the caster supports according to the manufacturer's instructions. (Also see "Tips.") Locate the casters as far apart from one another as possible, checking to see that they won't strike adjacent wooden parts as they swivel. Install the casters.

30. Finish the various parts in any way you wish. The project shown in the photo was finished with latex primer and latex enamel paints.

31. Bore two 1/16" pilot holes, each 3/4" deep, for the two screw eyes in the flag pole, locating them 1" and 24-1/2" from the top of the pole. Install the screw eyes in the holes, aligning the eyes with one another.

32. Cut the flag to size. Fold the longer edge over and sew it down to create a 1/2" slot. Slip the 1/8" rope through one screw eye, through the slot in the flag, and through the second screw eye. Tie a knot just above the flag and just below it. Then tie the two ends of the rope to each other to form a continuous loop. The flag can now be raised or lowered by pulling the rope. Seal the ends of the rope with plastic tape.

33. Slip the 3/4" rope through the anchor and through the anchor-line hole. Tie a knot at one end, inside the hatch, and at the other end to keep the anchor from slipping off. Seal the rope's ends with plastic tape. Now, watch your kids weigh anchor and head for the open sea!

BARGE

●●●●

This easy addition to the Tuggy Boat
project also functions on its own
as mobile toy storage.

CUT LIST

2 Sides • 3/4" x 8" x 22-1/2" plywood
2 Ends • 3/4" x 5-1/2" x 16" plywood
1 Bottom • 3/4" x 15" x 16" plywood
2 Caster supports • 3/4" x 1-1/2" x 16"

HARDWARE AND SUPPLIES

32 1-5/8" deck screws
10 1-1/4" deck screws
4 2" twin-wheel, stem-type, 75-lb. load rating casters
3 2-1/16" medium screw eyes
1 Medium S-hook
1 44" length of 1/2" nylon rope
  Plastic tape

SUGGESTED TOOLS

Layout tools
Circular saw
Jigsaw with scrolling blade
Claw hammer
3/8" drill
11/64" twist-drill bit
3/8" bradpoint bit
Pilot bits for 1-1/4" and 1-5/8" deck screws
Router with 3/8" rounding-over bit
Pad sander

TIPS

• *Build this project from hardwood plywood and hardwood lumber. For outdoor use, purchase pressure-treated plywood and lumber and use exterior-grade finishes.*

• *For tips on installing the casters, see the "Tips" section in the Tuggy Boat project on page 83.*

• *If you'll be building the Barge as a solo project (without the Tuggy Boat), you won't need to purchase the screw eyes, S-hook, or nylon rope. See Steps 14 through 16 for details.*

INSTRUCTIONS

1. Lay out the sides and ends on 3/4" plywood stock.

2. Enlarge the cutting pattern for the sides and transfer it (twice) to two 8" x 22-1/2" pieces of 3/4" plywood stock, making sure to transfer all hole locations as well.

3. Cut out all the plywood pieces, using your circular saw and your jigsaw and scrolling blade. Note that once you've cut the radii on the corners of the side pieces, their longest dimension will be 21-1/8".

4. Mark and cut the two caster supports to length.

5. Centered across the outside face of each caster support, lay out and bore a row of five pilot holes for 1-1/4" deck screws, 3-1/2" apart.

BARGE

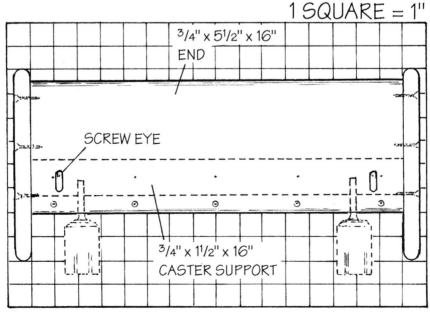

1 SQUARE = 1"

3/4" x 5 1/2" x 16"
END

SCREW EYE

3/4" x 1 1/2" x 16"
CASTER SUPPORT

END VIEW

6. On the outside face of each end piece, lay out and bore a row of five pilot holes for 1-5/8" deck screws, 3-1/2" apart and 3/8" in from an edge.

7. On the outside face of each side piece, lay out and bore eleven pilot holes for 1-5/8" deck screws, as shown in the cutting pattern.

8. Temporarily clamp together all the wooden parts and mark the arrises for routing. (Avoid arrises that will meet after assembly.) Disassemble the parts and use your router and 3/8" rounding-over bit to rout the marked arrises.

9. Sand all parts thoroughly.

10. Using 1-5/8" deck screws, attach the two end pieces to the bottom piece.

11. Attach the two side pieces to this assembly, also using 1-5/8" deck screws.

12. Use 1-1/4" deck screws to fasten the two caster supports to the inside faces of the end pieces.

13. Lay out a 3/8" caster-socket hole in each corner of the underside of the bottom piece, 3/8" from a 16" edge and 2-1/8" from a 15" end. Before boring the holes, hold a caster to one hole to make sure that it won't bump the inside face of the side piece when it swivels; adjust the hole positions as necessary. Then use your 3/8" bradpoint bit to bore the holes.

14. You'll need a tow line to attach the Barge to the Tuggy Boat project. Using an 11/64" twist-drill bit, bore two pilot holes for screw eyes in the Barge's front end; locate these holes 1-1/2" up from the bottom edge and 1-1/4" in from each end. Then bore a pilot hole centered along the hatch back of the Tuggy Boat, 3/8" above its lowest edge. (Avoid hitting any screws you may have installed here already.)

15. Using slip-joint pliers, install the three screw eyes.

16. Tape the ends of the nylon rope so that they won't unravel and knot the ends onto the Barge's screw eyes. Then slip the doubled rope over one end of the S-hook and knot the doubled section close to the hook to secure the rope. For towing, slip the S-hook over the Tuggy Boat's screw eye.

17. After touch-up sanding, finish the project with latex primer and latex enamel paints or with any other finish you prefer.

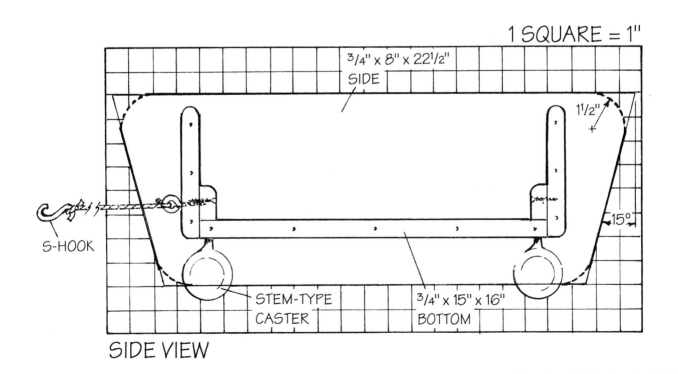

1 SQUARE = 1"

3/4" x 8" x 22¹/2"
SIDE

1¹/2"

15°

S-HOOK

STEM-TYPE CASTER

3/4" x 15" x 16"
BOTTOM

SIDE VIEW

HOPPYTOAD ROCKER

●●●●

*Two can play on this
easy-to-build teeter-totter.*

CUT LIST

1 Seat • 1-1/2" x 9-1/4" x 40"
1 Center brace • 1-1/2" x 9-1/4" x 7"
2 Side braces • 1-1/2" x 9-1/4" x 7-1/2" (long point)
2 Sides • 3/4" x 16" x 22" birch plywood
2 Handles • 1" x 11-3/4" dowel

HARDWARE AND SUPPLIES

30 1-1/4" deck screws
4 1-5/8" deck screws

SUGGESTED TOOLS

Layout tools
Backsaw and miter box
Circular saw
Jigsaw with medium-toothed and scrolling blades
Rasps
Claw hammer
No. 2 Phillips screwdriver
3/8" drill
1" bradpoint bit
Pilot bits for 1-1/4" and 1-5/8" deck screws
Router with 3/8" rounding-over bit
Pad sander

TIPS

- *If your kids will be playing with this project outdoors, use wooden materials that are treated and
finished to resist decay.*

- *For an attractive painted appearance, recess all
screws, fill them, and sand them flat.*

SIDE LAYOUT

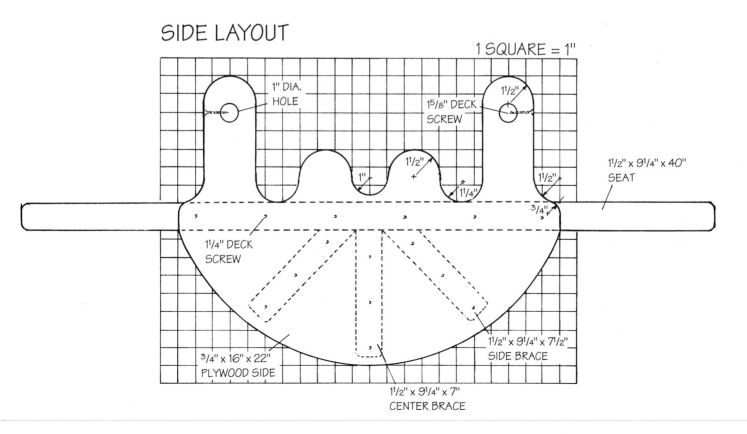

1 SQUARE = 1"

1" DIA. HOLE

1⁵/₈" DECK SCREW

1¹/₂" x 9¹/₄" x 40" SEAT

1¹/₄" DECK SCREW

³/₄" x 16" x 22" PLYWOOD SIDE

1¹/₂" x 9¹/₄" x 7¹/₂" SIDE BRACE

1¹/₂" x 9¹/₄" x 7" CENTER BRACE

HOPPYTOAD ROCKER

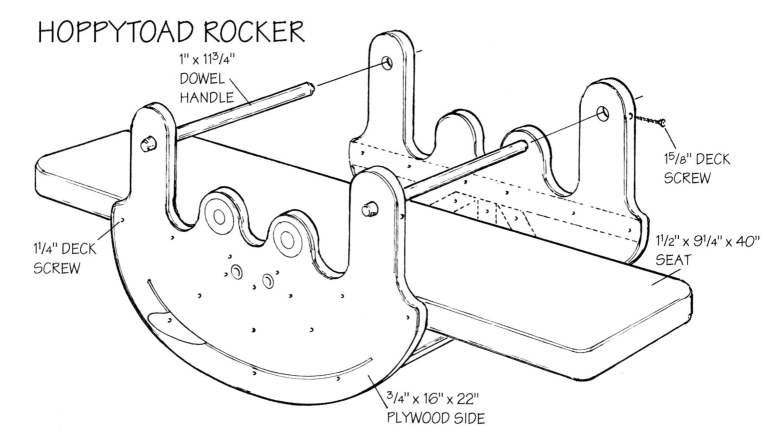

1" x 11³/₄"
DOWEL
HANDLE

1⁵/₈" DECK
SCREW

1¹/₄" DECK
SCREW

1¹/₂" x 9¹/₄" x 40"
SEAT

³/₄" x 16" x 22"
PLYWOOD SIDE

INSTRUCTIONS

1. Enlarge the side-piece cutting pattern and transfer it (twice) onto the bottom faces of the plywood pieces. Be sure to transfer all boring locations as well.

2. Cut out the shapes with your jigsaw, using a medium-toothed blade for straight lines and broad curves and the scrolling blade for tight curves.

3. Lay out and bore the 1"-diameter through-holes for the handles.

4. Using your rasps, carefully smooth the edges of both side pieces.

5. Lay out the seat and the three braces on the 1-1/2" stock, noting the 45-degree cuts on one end of each side brace. Cut the pieces to length.

6. Mark a 1-1/4" radius at each corner of the seat. Then cut all four radii with your jigsaw and scrolling blade.

7. Dry-clamp the various parts together temporarily. (An extra pair of hands is a big help here!) Mark the arrises that need easing, avoiding those areas where parts meet. To help prevent pinched toes, be sure to include the arrises on the bottom edges of the three braces.

8. After disassembling the parts, use a 3/8" rounding-over bit in your router to ease the marked arrises.

9. With your backsaw and miter box, cut the dowel handles to length. Then rasp each end to a 1/2" radius.

10. Bore the fifteen pilot holes for 1-1/4" deck screws in each side piece; all should be counterbored 1/16".

11. Thoroughly sand all parts.

12. Fasten the sides to the seat with 1-1/4" deck screws. Then install the three braces with the remaining 1-1/4" screws.

13. Insert the handles in the paired holes so that a radiused end protrudes from each plywood face. Then, in the edges of each side piece, mark and bore two 1-5/8" pilot holes to pierce the handles, counterboring these holes 1/16".

14. To secure the handles in place, install a 1-5/8" deck screw in each hole.

15. Fill all counterbores with wood filler and sand them flat when the filler has dried.

16. After removing all traces of sawdust, prime all parts and let them dry.

17. Using the photo as a guide, paint the Hoppytoad Rocker with bright colors. Rock on!

LITTLE RED WAGON

● ● ● ●

Here's the all-time greatest carry-all.

CUT LIST

2 Long sides • 3/4" x 3-1/2" x 25-1/2"
2 Front and back • 3/4" x 3-1/2" x 13-1/2"
2 High sides • 3/4" x 3-1/2" x 15"
1 High back • 3/4" x 3-1/2" x 13-1/2"
9 Connectors • 3/8" x 1-1/2" dowel
2 Long bottom supports • 1/2" x 3/4" x 24"
2 Short bottom supports • 3/4" x 3-1/2" x 12-1/2"
1 Bottom • 5/8" x 13-1/2" x 24" plywood
1 Handle support • 3/4" x 2-1/2" x 2-1/2"
1 Handle shaft • 1" x 22" dowel
1 Handle • 1-1/4" x 3-3/4" dowel

SUGGESTED TOOLS

Layout tools
Backsaw and miter box
Circular saw
Jigsaw with scrolling blade
Claw hammer
3/8" drill
11/64" twist-drill bit
1/8", 3/8", and 1" bradpoint bits
Pilot bits for 1", 1-1/4", and 1-5/8" deck screws
Bit sized to bore caster-mounting holes
Router with chamfer bit adjusted for 3/16" cut
Pad sander

HARDWARE AND SUPPLIES

12 1" deck screws
41 1-1/4" deck screws
8 1-5/8" deck screws
2 2-1/16" medium screw eyes
2 4" plate-type casters
2 4" plate-type swivel casters

TIPS

- *If mounting screws aren't included with your casters, ask a salesperson to give you a hand selecting them.*
- *If 1-1/4" dowel isn't available, ask for a product known as* closet rod.

LITTLE RED WAGON

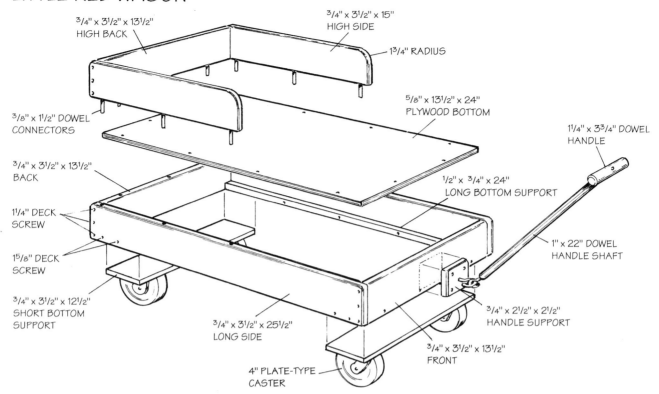

³/4" x 3¹/2" x 13¹/2"
HIGH BACK

³/4" x 3¹/2" x 15"
HIGH SIDE

1³/4" RADIUS

⁵/8" x 13¹/2" x 24"
PLYWOOD BOTTOM

1¹/4" x 3³/4" DOWEL
HANDLE

³/8" x 1¹/2" DOWEL
CONNECTORS

³/4" x 3¹/2" x 13¹/2"
BACK

1¹/4" DECK
SCREW

1⁵/8" DECK
SCREW

³/4" x 3¹/2" x 12¹/2"
SHORT BOTTOM
SUPPORT

¹/2" x ³/4" x 24"
LONG BOTTOM SUPPORT

1" x 22" DOWEL
HANDLE SHAFT

³/4" x 3¹/2" x 25¹/2"
LONG SIDE

³/4" x 2¹/2" x 2¹/2"
HANDLE SUPPORT

³/4" x 3¹/2" x 13¹/2"
FRONT

4" PLATE-TYPE
CASTER

INSTRUCTIONS

1. Lay out all parts and cut them to size, using your backsaw and miter box to cut the dowel parts.

2. Mark a 1-3/4" radius on one corner of each high side. Then cut the radii with your jigsaw.

3. Centered across the top edge of each long side, lay out three 3/8" holes for dowel connectors; locate them 1", 7-1/2", and 14" from an end. Then transfer identical marks onto the bottom (flat) edges of the high sides.

4. Using your 3/8" bradpoint bit and a stop collar adjusted for a 5/8" depth, bore the twelve holes.

5. Repeat Steps 3 and 4 with the back and high back, locating the holes 1-1/4", 6-3/4", and 12-1/4" from one end of each piece.

6. In one face of both the front and back pieces, lay out and bore three pilot holes for 1-1/4" deck screws. Locate the holes 3/8" from the bottom edge and 1-3/4", 6-3/4", and 11-3/4" from one end.

7. On one face of each long side, lay out and bore two sets of three pilot holes for 1-1/4" deck screws, locating each set 3/8" from an end and 1/2", 1-3/4", and 3" from an edge. On the same face of each, also bore four pilot holes for 1-5/8" deck screws, 3/8"

from the bottom edge and 1-1/8", 2-7/8", 22-3/8", and 24-3/8" from an end.

8. On each high side, bore three pilot holes for 1-1/4" deck screws; locate them 3/8" from the square end and 1/2", 1-3/4", and 3" from an edge.

9. In each corner of the handle support, bore a pilot hole for a 1-1/4" deck screw; locate each hole 1/2" in from adjacent edges.

10. In each long bottom support, bore three pilot holes for 1" deck screws, centering the holes across the 3/4" face, 6-1/2", 12", and 17-1/2" from an end.

11. Using the diagram and photo as a guide, mark the arrises for routing, avoiding arrises that meet. Then, with your router and a chamfer bit adjusted for a 3/16" cut, rout the arrises.

12. Sand all parts thoroughly.

13. Form a rectangular box shape by fastening the two long sides onto the ends of the front and back pieces; use three 1-1/4" deck screws at each joint.

14. Use glue and 1" deck screws to attach the two long bottom supports to the inside faces of the long sides. Be sure that the bottom edges of the supports and sides are flush.

15. Place the two short bottom supports between the long bottom supports, fitting their outer edges tightly against the front and back pieces. Secure the pieces with 1-1/4" deck screws driven through the front and back and 1-5/8" deck screws driven through the long sides.

16. Set the plywood bottom in place inside the box shape and bore a dozen pilot holes for 1-1/4" deck screws as follows: two holes 3/8" in from each end and 4" and 9-1/2" from an edge; and four holes 1/4" in from each edge and 2", 8-3/4", 15-1/2", and 22" from an end. Fasten the bottom in position with 1-1/4" screws.

17. Fasten the two high sides onto the ends of the high back, using three 1-1/4" deck screws at each joint.

18. Glue the nine 3/8" dowel connectors into their holes in the lower assembly, tapping gently to seat each dowel.

19. Apply a drop or two of glue to each 3/8" hole in the high-sides-and-back assembly. Then attach this assembly to the protruding connectors by tapping gently until the facing edges are 1/4" apart.

20. Center the handle support across the front piece's length and width and attach it with glue and 1-1/4" deck screws.

21. Bore a centered 11/64" hole, 1-1/4" deep, in the face of the handle support.

22. Secure the handle and bore a centered 1" hole, 3/4" deep, in its curved edge, 1-7/8" from an end.

23. Using your 1/8" bit, bore through the center of the 1" hole so that the bit's tip pierces the curved outer edge of the handle. Then, using a pilot bit for a 1-1/4" deck screw, bore a slightly countersunk pilot hole by inserting the bit into the handle's outer edge, centering it in the 1/8" hole.

24. Attach the handle to the handle shaft with glue and a 1-1/4" deck screw.

25. Bore a 1/8" hole, 1-1/4" deep, in the center of the free end of the handle shaft.

26. Install screw eyes in the handle support and in the end of the handle shaft. Open one eye with pliers, slip it over the other eye, and close the open eye to connect the two together. Adjust the eyes' positions to allow for free movement of the handle when the wagon is in use.

27. Use sandpaper to touch up any rough edges. Remove the sanding dust.

28. Finish the wagon in any way you wish. The project shown in the photo was primed and painted with latex enamel finishes.

29. Install the two fixed casters on the rear corners of the wagon's bottom and the two swivel casters on its front corners. (Be sure to pilot bore all screw locations.)

SHOPPING CART

●●●●

Attention young shoppers!
Special bargains on aisle number nine!

CUT LIST

- 2 Sides • 3/4" x 15-3/4" x 21-1/4" plywood
- 1 Bottom • 3/4" x 9" x 11" plywood
- 2 Seat and seat back • 3/4" x 4-3/8" x 9" plywood
- 1 Handle • 1" x 11-1/2" dowel
- 13 Braces • 5/8" x 9-3/4" dowel
- 1 Small brace • 3/8" x 5-3/8" dowel
- 2 Axle • 5/8" x 13" dowel
- 4 Wheels (Type A) • 3/4" x 4"-diameter plywood

HARDWARE AND SUPPLIES

- 25 1-1/4" deck screws
- 4 8d finishing nails
- 4 3/4" cut washers

SUGGESTED TOOLS

Layout tools
Circular saw
Jigsaw with plywood blade
Rasps
Claw hammer
3/8" drill
5/8", 11/16", and 1" bradpoint bits
1/16" twist-drill bit
Pilot bit for 1-1/4" deck screws
Router with chamfer bit adjusted for 1/8" cut
        and 3/8" rounding-over bit
Pad sander

TIPS

- *Use hardwood plywood for all plywood parts.*
- *To assemble this project, you'll need four bar clamps with minimum jaw openings of 10-5/8".*

SHOPPING CART

1 SQUARE = 1"

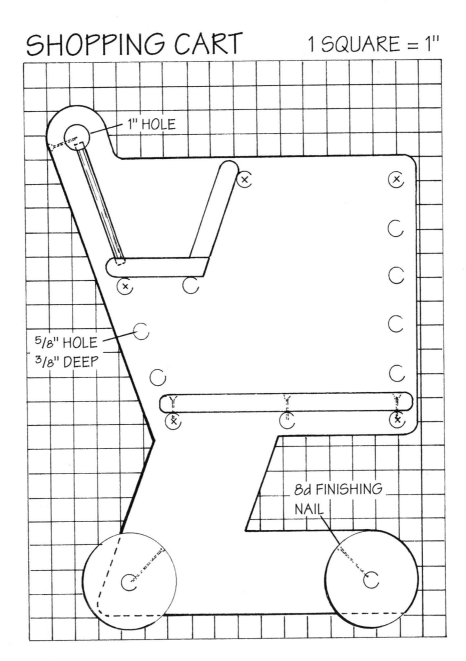

1" HOLE

5/8" HOLE
3/8" DEEP

8d FINISHING
NAIL

INSTRUCTIONS

1. Enlarge the cutting pattern for the sides and transfer it (twice) to the appropriate stock. Also transfer the hole locations.

2. Cut the plywood parts out, using your circular saw and your jigsaw and plywood blade; note the 20-degree bevel cuts on one edge of the seat and seat back. Also lay out and cut the dowel parts to length.

3. With your center finder, locate the center of each wheel and bore a 5/8" hole through it.

4. Bore the sixteen marked holes in each side piece, using your 5/8" bit for the thirteen 3/8"-deep brace holes, your 11/16" bit for the two axle through-holes, and your 1" bit for the handle through-hole.

5. Use your router and a chamfer bit adjusted for a 1/8" cut to rout all arrises of the side pieces.

6. Switch to a 3/8" rounding-over bit to rout the square 9" arrises of the seat and seat back and the 9" arrises of the bottom piece. Avoid routing the beveled edges.

7. On the narrower face of the seat, bore three pilot holes for 1-1/4" deck screws, angling them at 20 degrees to match the angle of the seat back. Locate these holes 1", 4-1/2", and 8" from one end and 3/8" from the beveled edge.

8. Fasten the seat parts together with three 1-1/4" deck screws to form a slanted, L-shaped assembly.

9. Using clamps, assemble the sides, the cross braces, and the bottom piece; don't use any glue at this stage.

10. Bore the five pilot holes for 1-1/4" deck screws in the outside face of each side piece. (In the diagram, each of these locations is marked with an X.)

11. Mark the points where the sides meet the bottom piece and where the three cross braces under the bottom piece touch the bottom piece's bottom face.

12. Remove the bottom from the assembly and bore three pairs of pilot holes for 1-1/4" deck screws in its top face; locate these holes 1" in from the ends and center each pair directly over a marked cross-brace location. Reclamp the bottom piece in place.

13. Place the seat assembly in its proper location. Then bore a pair of pilot holes for 1-1/4" deck screws in the upper face of the seat and in the upper face of the seat back. Locate these holes to pierce the dowel cross brace behind each piece.

14. Bore a 3/8" hole, 5/16" deep, in the upper face of the seat, centering it 5/8" from the rounded front edge and angling it at 70 degrees above the horizontal seat.

15. Bore another 3/8" hole, 5/16" deep, into the curved edge of the handle, centering the hole along the handle's length and across its thickness.

16. Use your flat rasp to create radii on the ends of the axles and handle.

17. Insert the handle into the matching 1" holes in the sides; each end should project an equal distance beyond each side. Test-fit the small brace in the handle and seat. With the brace in position, bore a pilot hole for a 1-1/4" deck screw in the edge of each side piece, adjacent to the handle. The bit should pierce the center of the handle's thickness at each location.

18. After taking the assembly apart, thoroughly sand all parts and remove the sanding dust.

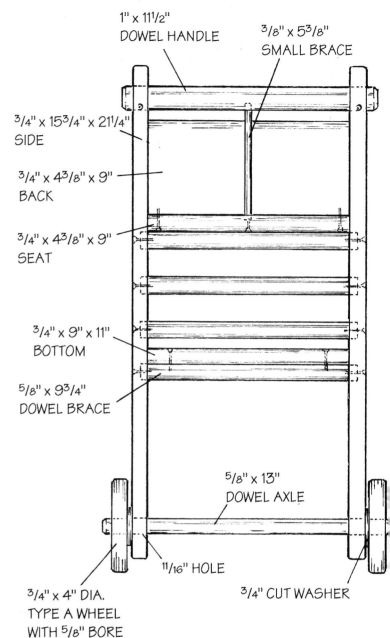

1" x 11 1/2" DOWEL HANDLE

3/8" x 5 3/8" SMALL BRACE

3/4" x 15 3/4" x 21 1/4" SIDE

3/4" x 4 3/8" x 9" BACK

3/4" x 4 3/8" x 9" SEAT

3/4" x 9" x 11" BOTTOM

5/8" x 9 3/4" DOWEL BRACE

5/8" x 13" DOWEL AXLE

11/16" HOLE

3/4" x 4" DIA. TYPE A WHEEL WITH 5/8" BORE

3/4" CUT WASHER

19. Finish the project as you wish. The cart in the photo was primed with latex primer and painted with latex enamel paints.

20. Assemble your Shopping Cart with deck screws. Slide the axles through the paired 11/16" holes in the side pieces. Slip a washer and wheel over each axle end, allowing 3/32" "wiggle room" between each washer and plywood face. Fasten the wheels to the axles with 8d finishing nails (see page 39).

CLASSIC HOBBYHORSE

● ● ● ●

Wheeled toys from yesteryear never go out of style, and this pony proves it!

CUT LIST

1   Head center • 3/4" x 8-1/2" x 9-3/4"
2   Head sides • 3/4" x 5-5/8" x 11-1/4"
1   Shaft • 1-1/4" x 31" dowel
2   Wheels • 3/4" x 4-1/4"-diameter

HARDWARE AND SUPPLIES

1   1-1/4" deck screw
2   No. 18 x 1/2" wire nails
1   1/2" (O.D.) x 3-1/4" steel tubing
1   3/8" x 3-7/8" brass threaded rod
4   1/2" cut washers
1   1/4" cut washer
2   3/8" locking washers
2   3/8" brass cap nuts
1   Cotton mop head
1   36" length of 3/4" decorative ribbon

SUGGESTED TOOLS

Layout tools
Backsaw and miter box
Jigsaw with medium-toothed and scrolling blades
Rasps
Claw hammer
No. 2 Phillips screwdriver
3/8" drill
1/2", 9/16", and 1-1/4" bradpoint bits
1/16" twist-drill bit
Router with 3/8" rounding-over bit
    and chamfer bit adjusted for 1/8" cut
Pad sander

TIPS

• *A dozen adjustable clamps or C-clamps are helpful for clamping the three head pieces together.*
• *You'll find the decorative ribbon at a fabrics store.*

CLASSIC HOBBYHORSE

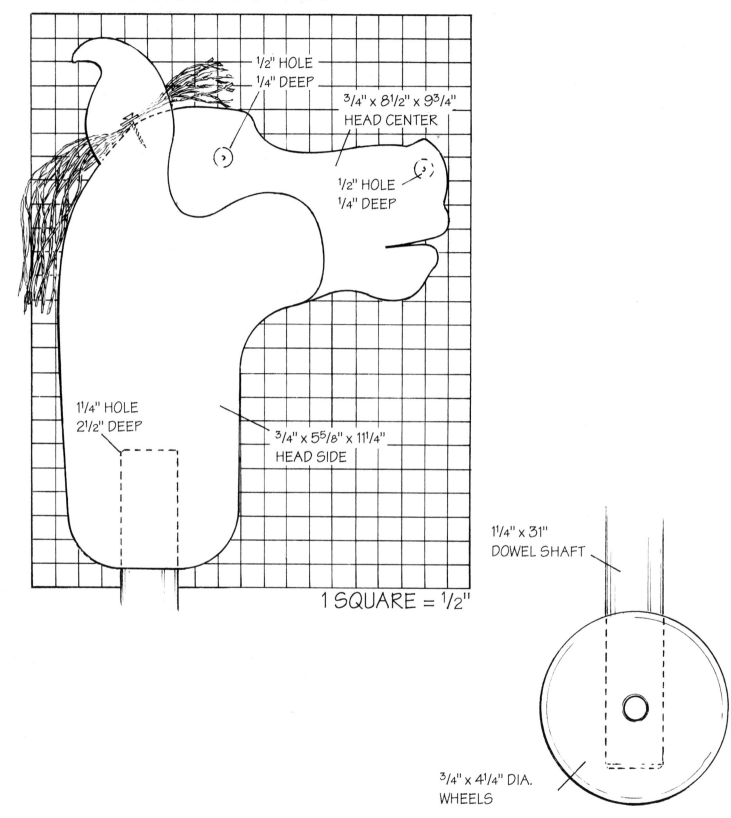

1/2" HOLE
1/4" DEEP

3/4" x 8¹/2" x 9³/4"
HEAD CENTER

1/2" HOLE
1/4" DEEP

1¹/4" HOLE
2¹/2" DEEP

3/4" x 5⁵/8" x 11¹/4"
HEAD SIDE

1 SQUARE = 1/2"

1¹/4" x 31"
DOWEL SHAFT

3/4" x 4¹/4" DIA.
WHEELS

INSTRUCTIONS

1. Enlarge the patterns for the head center and two head sides and transfer them, including the mouth, eye, and nostril locations, to 3/4" stock.

2. Cut out the three shapes with your jigsaw and scrolling blade; then cut the mouth into the head center.

3. Using your 1/2" bit, bore the eye holes and nostrils to 1/4" depths on each face of the head center.

4. Secure each head side and, using your router and 3/8" rounding-over bit, round over the arrises.

5. Temporarily clamp the head sides to the head center, aligning the edges carefully, and mark the visible arrises of the head center for routing. Remove the clamps.

6. Secure the center piece. Then, using your router and 3/8" rounding-over bit, rout the marked arrises.

7. Rasp and sand all three head pieces thoroughly.

8. Spread some glue on the inside faces of the head sides. Clamp them onto the head center, aligning them carefully, and let the assembly dry thoroughly. (Peel off any glue squeeze-out while it's partially dried and still rubbery.)

9. Secure the assembly so that the bottom of the neck faces up and lay out the centered 1-1/4" hole for the shaft.

10. Bore the 1-1/4" hole, 2-1/2" deep, taking care to hold the drill as straight as possible.

11. Rasp and sand the head assembly, smoothing joint lines and other trouble spots carefully.

12. Lay out the 1-1/4" shaft to 31" in length and use your backsaw and miter box to cut it to size.

13. Lay out and bore a 1/2"-diameter through-hole for the steel axle, centering the hole 1-1/4" from one end of the shaft.

14. With your compass, lay out two 4-1/4"-diameter wheels on 3/4" stock. Carefully cut out the circles, using your jigsaw and medium-toothed blade (see page 37).

15. With your center finder, determine the exact center of each wheel. After marking these centers, secure the wheels and bore a 9/16" through-hole at each mark.

16. Using your router fitted with a chamfer bit, carefully rout a 1/8" chamfer on each radiused arris of each wheel.

17. Sand the shaft and wheels thoroughly.

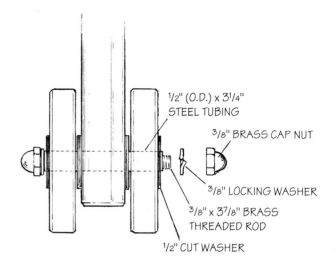

1/2" (O.D.) x 3¼"
STEEL TUBING

3/8" BRASS CAP NUT

3/8" LOCKING WASHER

3/8" x 3⅞" BRASS
THREADED ROD

1/2" CUT WASHER

18. Finish the head assembly, shaft, and wheels with water-based satin varnish. Apply at least two coats, sanding between applications and letting each coat dry thoroughly. Then, if you wish, detail the eyes with latex enamel paint.

19. To construct the wheel assembly, first use a hacksaw to cut the threaded rod to 3-7/8" in length and the 1/2" O.D. steel tubing to 3-1/4" in length (see page 39).

20. Gently drive the tubing through the 1/2" hole in the shaft so that an equal length protrudes from each side. Slide the threaded rod through the tubing and slip a 1/2" cut washer over each end. Then add the wheels and finish the assembly by adding the 1/2" cut washers, the locking washers, and the cap nuts. Using an adjustable wrench, tighten the cap nuts well.

21. Apply glue to the 1-1/4" hole in the head assembly and press or drive the shaft into the hole, aligning the head with the wheels.

22. To complete your project, first cut a 3" or 4" section from the mop head. Then cut the individual fabric strands to different lengths in order to make the mop look like a mane. To attach the mane between the horse's ears, drive a deck screw through a 1/4" cut washer and on through the center of the fabric backing into the back of the horse's head.

23. To attach the horse's reins, fasten the fabric ribbon to the head (see photo), using a wire nail on each side.

LUGE

● ● ● ●

This mini-toboggan thrilled fans at the Winter Olympics, and your kids will love it too.

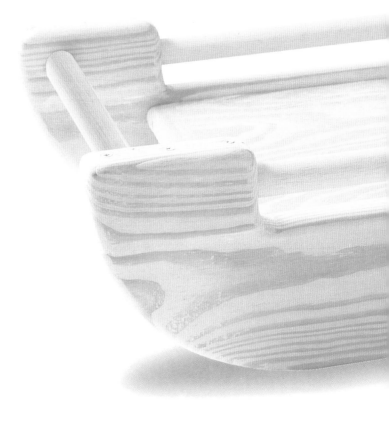

CUT LIST

1 Deck • 3/4" x 12" x 27" plywood
2 End caps • 3/4" x 1" x 12"
2 Deck supports • 3/4" x 3/4" x 27"
2 Runners • 1-1/2" x 7-1/4" x 36"
2 Grips • 1" x 28" dowel
1 Bar • 1" x 13" dowel

HARDWARE AND SUPPLIES

6 3" deck screws
10 1-5/8" deck screws
40 1-1/4" deck screws
4 2-1/2" galvanized angle braces
1 5' length of 3/8" braided nylon cord

SUGGESTED TOOLS

Layout tools
Backsaw and miter box
Circular saw with rip fence
Jigsaw with medium-toothed and scrolling blades
Block plane
Rasps
Claw hammer
No. 2 Phillips screwdriver
3/8" drill
1" bradpoint bit
1/16" twist-drill bit
Pilot bits for 1-1/4", 1-5/8", and 3" deck screws
Pilot bit to match angle-brace screws
Router with 1/4" and 3/8" rounding-over bits
Pad sander

TIPS

- *Purchase pressure-treated plywood and lumber for this outdoors project; clear, straight-grained lumber is best. Because pressure-treated dowels are not commonly available, dowel parts should be finished to resist moisture and fungi.*

- *Before cutting out the runners, it's helpful to understand that each one is cut into two sections: a toe (see the upper right-hand section of the assembly diagram) and the remaining section of the runner. The toes are cut as separate pieces so that you can install the grips and then glue the toes back onto the runners. Use a circular-saw rip fence to ensure an accurate cut and a tight glue joint.*

- *To secure the glued-up runners, you'll need several clamps with a jaw opening at least 7-1/4" wide.*

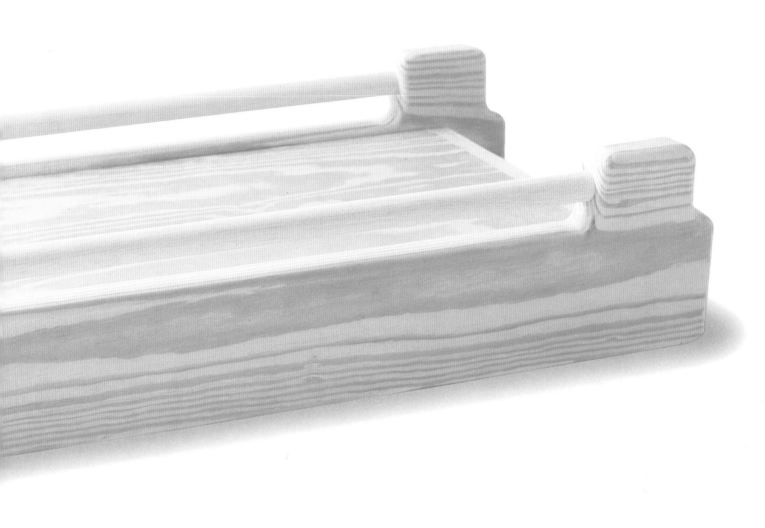

INSTRUCTIONS

1. Enlarge the cutting pattern for the runner and transfer it (twice) to the face of the 1-1/2" stock; be sure to transfer all boring locations as well.

2. To cut out the runners, first use your circular saw and rip fence to make a 29-1/2"-long rip cut, 4-3/4" from the bottom of each runner layout, starting from the front of each runner layout and extending toward its back. Note that your circular-saw blade will remove about 1/8" of the runner's width at the toe end.

3. With your jigsaw, cut out all the remaining layouts on both runners, except for the 6-1/2" radii; leave the stock the full 7-1/4" width for now.

4. To maintain an equal width at the toe and heel of each finished runner, use your block plane to remove approximately 1/8" of stock from the top of each

runner's heel. This will compensate for the thickness of the circular-saw blade that you used in Step 2.

5. After laying out the three dowel parts, cut them to length with your backsaw and miter box.

6. Secure the runners and toe pieces for boring. Using a 1" bradpoint bit flagged for a 1" depth, bore a 1" hole on the inner edge of each toe and on the inner edge of each heel; see the cutting pattern for these hole locations. Keep the holes as straight as possible.

7. Insert one end of a dowel grip in the hole in one runner's heel. Then slip the other end into the hole in a toe piece. Apply some glue at the ripped joint and clamp the toe and runner together. Repeat with the parts of the second runner. Allow both assemblies to dry.

LUGE

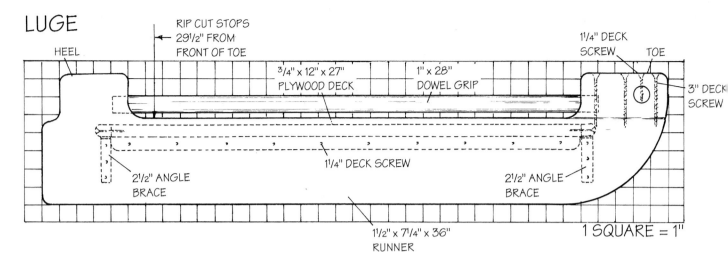

HEEL

RIP CUT STOPS 29½" FROM FRONT OF TOE

¾" x 12" x 27" PLYWOOD DECK

1" x 28" DOWEL GRIP

1¼" DECK SCREW   TOE

3" DECK SCREW

1¼" DECK SCREW

2½" ANGLE BRACE

2½" ANGLE BRACE

1½" x 7¼" x 36" RUNNER

1 SQUARE = 1"

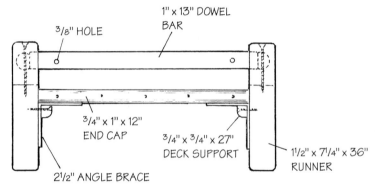

3/8" HOLE

1" x 13" DOWEL BAR

¾" x 1" x 12" END CAP

¾" x ¾" x 27" DECK SUPPORT

1½" x 7¼" x 36" RUNNER

2½" ANGLE BRACE

8. To prevent the grips from rotating and to further secure the glued joints, bore three pilot holes for 3" deck screws in the top edge of each toe (see diagram). Then install the screws in the holes.

9. With your jigsaw, cut the 6-1/2" radii on the bottom front corners of the runners.

10. Bore a 1"-diameter, 1/2"-deep bar hole in the inside face of each runner.

11. Lay out the plywood deck, the two end caps, and the two deck supports and cut them to size with your circular saw. The rip fence is useful when ripping thin pieces such as the supports.

12. In two adjacent faces of each deck support, mark and bore pilot holes for 1-1/4" deck screws, 3" apart, staggering the holes in each face so that the inserted screws won't meet.

13. In the outer face of each end cap, bore pilot holes for 1-5/8" deck screws, spacing them 2-1/2" apart.

14. Using your router and 1/4" rounding-over bit, ease the two arrises of each end cap that are on the side from which you bored the pilot holes. Also ease the inside bottom arrises and ends of the deck supports.

15. Apply some glue to the inner edge of each end cap. Then, using 1-5/8" screws, secure the caps at opposite ends of the deck, aligning the ends and edges carefully.

16. Chuck a 3/8" rounding-over bit in your router and ease all arrises on the two runners; use your rasp wherever the router bit can't reach.

17. Mark and bore the two 3/8" through-holes in the bar.

18. Carefully sand all parts.

19. Using glue and 1-1/4" screws, attach the deck supports to the inside faces of the runners, locating the eased arrises to face the bottoms of the runners.

20. Fasten the lower face of the deck to the upper face of one deck support, using 1-1/4" deck screws inserted through the deck supports. Then slip the 1" dowel bar into the holes in both runners and fasten the second runner to the deck.

21. To secure the bar, bore a pilot hole for a 1-1/4" deck screw into the top edge of each runner toe; the bit should pierce the dowel bar. Then install a 1-1/4" deck screw in each hole.

22. Lay out the locations for the angle braces' mounting screws according to the manufacturer's instructions and, after boring the pilot holes for the screws, install the hardware.

23. Finish all parts with water-resistant, exterior-grade finishes. Knot the braided cord through the bar's holes and you're all set!

SCOOTER

●●●●

This scorcher is a kid's second-best friend!

CUT LIST

1 Base • 3/4" x 5-1/2" x 26"
2 Uprights • 3/4" x 5" x 24"
1 Top brace • 3/4" x 1-1/2" x 13-1/2"
1 Center brace • 1-1/2" x 2-1/2" x 7"
1 Cross brace • 1-1/2" x 2-1/2" x 10-1/2"
2 Caster supports • 3/4" x 2-1/2" x 2-1/2"
1 Handle • 1" x 10" dowel

HARDWARE AND SUPPLIES

18 1-1/4" deck screws
11 1-5/8" deck screws
2 2" twin-wheel, 75-lb. load rating swivel casters
2 2" twin-wheel, 75-lb. load rating casters

SUGGESTED TOOLS

Layout tools
Backsaw and miter box
Circular saw
Jigsaw with scrolling blade
Paring and firmer chisels
Rasps
Claw hammer
3/8" drill
1" bradpoint bit
Pilot bits for 1-1/4" and 1-5/8" deck screws
Bit sized to bore caster-mounting holes
Router with chamfer bit adjusted for 3/16" cut
Pad sander

TIP

• *If the casters don't include mounting screws, ask a salesperson for a hand selecting the appropriate hardware.*

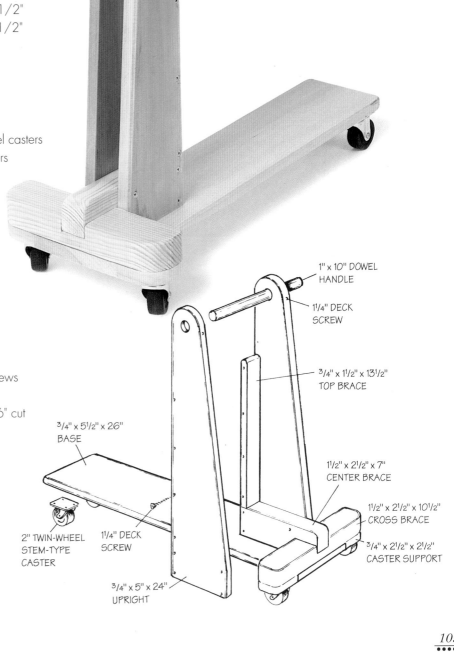

1" x 10" DOWEL HANDLE

1¼" DECK SCREW

3/4" x 1½" x 13½" TOP BRACE

1½" x 2½" x 7" CENTER BRACE

1½" x 2½" x 10½" CROSS BRACE

3/4" x 2½" x 2½" CASTER SUPPORT

3/4" x 5½" x 26" BASE

2" TWIN-WHEEL STEM-TYPE CASTER

1¼" DECK SCREW

3/4" x 5" x 24" UPRIGHT

INSTRUCTIONS

1. Lay out the base (including the eleven hole locations shown in the Base Screw Layout), the top brace, and the caster supports on one face of your 3/4" stock. Cut the pieces to length with your circular saw.

2. Use a rasp to round over the 1-1/2" arrises on one end of the top brace.

3. On each caster support, scribe a 1-1/4" radius on the front corner and a 1/2" radius on the adjacent rear corner. Cut the radii with your jigsaw and scrolling blade.

4. Enlarge and transfer the cutting pattern for the uprights, including all hole locations. Cut the pieces to size with your circular saw and jigsaw. Note that the 6-degree angles at the 5" ends of the uprights are trimmed to 90 degrees with a circular saw so that the cross brace's rear edge will fit squarely against the edge of each upright.

5. Bore the 1" through-hole in each upright.

6. Lay out the center brace and cross brace on 1-1/2" stock and cut out the two rectangular shapes.

7. To form a lap joint in the center and cross braces, first mark a 3/4"-deep x 2-1/2"-long notch on one corner of the center brace and cut out the notch.

8. Then lay out and cut a 1/2" radius on the corner adjacent to the notched end.

9. Lay out a centered 3/4"-deep x 1-1/2"-wide notch in the cross brace's top face. Cut the notch out by first sawing the 2-1/2"-long "cheeks" with your backsaw and then chiseling out the waste to form a flat-bottomed notch. Test-fit the two braces, removing wood as necessary for a good fit.

10. At each end of the cross brace, mark and cut a 1-1/4" and a 1/2" radius, one radius at each adjacent corner. (Note that these pairs of radii match the pairs on the caster supports.)

11. Mark the various parts for routing as shown in the diagram and photo, avoiding arrises that meet. Rout the arrises with your router and a chamfer bit adjusted for a 3/16" cut.

12. Glue and clamp the faces of the caster supports onto the bottom (unnotched) face of the cross brace; the radii should match.

13. Mark and cut the 10" dowel handle. Then ease the arrises on each end with a rasp.

14. Bore the eight pilot holes for 1-1/4" deck screws in the outside face of each upright. (Don't bore the pilot holes in the uprights' edges just yet.) Also bore the eleven pilot holes for 1-5/8" deck screws in the bottom face of the base.

15. Assemble the uprights and top brace, using deck screws inserted in the pilot holes. Next, assemble the base, center brace, and cross brace with caster supports, also using glue and screws. Then fasten the base assembly to the upright assembly.

16. Center the handle in the paired 1" holes in the uprights and bore a pilot hole for a 1-1/4" screw in the front edge of each upright so that the bit pierces the handle. Install a 1-1/4" deck screw in each hole.

17. Finish your project in any way you like.

18. Install the swivel casters on the caster supports' bottom faces, locating them as close to the outside edges as possible. Install the remaining two casters on the base piece's bottom face, as close to the end and edges as possible.

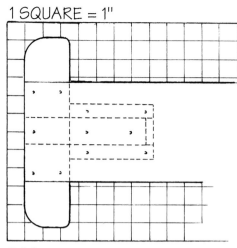

1 SQUARE = 1"

BASE SCREW DETAIL

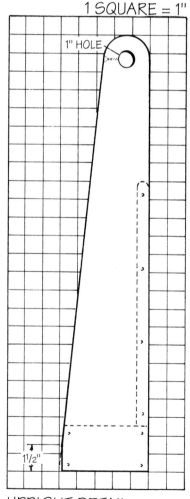

1 SQUARE = 1"

UPRIGHT DETAIL

FUN ROLLER

● ● ● ●

*Young children will invent their own play
with this easy-to-build project.*

CUT LIST

- 1 Base • 3/4" x 16"-diameter hardwood plywood
- 3 Grip supports • 3/4" x 2" x 2" hardwood plywood
- 3 Grips • 1" x 3-1/4" dowel

HARDWARE AND SUPPLIES

- 6 1-1/4" deck screws
- 3 1-5/8" deck screws
- 6 2" plate-type, 75-lb. load rating swivel casters

SUGGESTED TOOLS

Layout tools

Backsaw and miter box

Circular saw

Jigsaw with medium-toothed blade

Rasps

No. 2 Phillips screwdriver

3/8" drill

1" bradpoint bit

Pilot bits for 1-1/4" and 1-5/8" deck screws

Bit sized to bore caster-mounting holes

Router with 3/8" rounding-over bit

Pad sander

TIPS

- *Let your kids know that standing on this project, using it as a skateboard, and using it in high-traffic areas are all unsafe.*

- *The Fun Roller is only recommended for kids under 6 years of age and 60 pounds (.454 kg). For kids closer to the 6 year/60 pound limit, extend the base diameter to 18". Protective helmets, knee pads, and other body-protection gear are an excellent investment in your children's safety, and they look pretty cool, too!*

- *One easy way to lay out the circular base is to drive a 3d finishing nail into the face of the stock and tie a 9" piece of thin string onto the nail. Then tie the free end of the string to a pencil (near its point) so that the distance between the nail and the pencil point is exactly 8". To scribe the circle, just draw with the string held taut.*

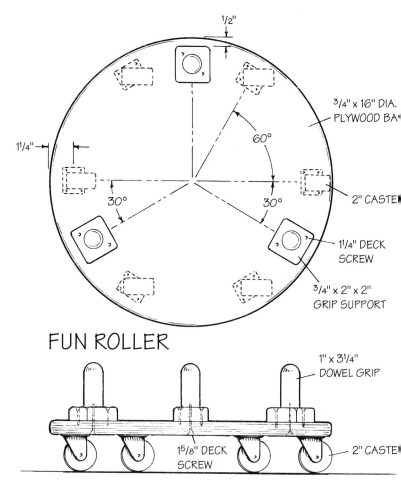

FUN ROLLER

INSTRUCTIONS

1. Lay out the 16"-diameter base on 3/4" hardwood plywood.

2. Cut the base out with your jigsaw and medium-toothed blade.

3. With your backsaw and miter box, cut the dowel grips to 3-1/4" lengths.

4. Lay out the four plywood grip supports and cut them out with your circular saw.

5. With your router and 3/8" rounding-over bit, round over both arrises of the base.

6. Mark the center of each grip support's face and bore a 1" through-hole at each mark.

7. Also bore two pilot holes for 1-1/4" deck screws in each grip support, locating them at opposite corners.

8. With your flat rasp, ease all arrises on the grip supports except those that will rest on the face of the base. Try to approximate the 3/8" round-over on the edge of the base. Also use your rasp to round over one end of each dowel grip.

9. Carefully sand all parts until they're smooth.

10. Using the diagram as a guide, mark locations for the grip supports on the top face of the base.

11. Turn the base over and mark positions for the casters and for pilot holes to accommodate the caster-mounting screws. On the same face, also mark pilot holes for the 1-5/8" screws that will secure the grips in the grip-support holes. Then bore the holes, using the appropriate pilot bits at each screw location.

12. Place a little glue on the square face of each grip support. Position each support on the base and secure it with two 1-1/4" deck screws.

13. Install the grips in the grip supports. Secure each one with a 1-5/8" deck screw driven through the bottom of the base.

14. Paint or finish the base assembly in any way you wish.

15. Install the casters on the bottom of the base.

GARDEN CART

• • • •

Gardening is lots of fun with this knee-high version of an outdoor classic.

HARDWARE AND SUPPLIES

18 1" deck screws
1 lb. 1-1/4" deck screws
6 1-5/8" deck screws
2 8" x 1.75 rubber-tire, ball-bearing wheels, (axle bore,1/2" diameter; hub length, 1-3/8")
1 18-5/16" x 1/2" O.D. steel tubing
1 18-13/16" x 3/8"-diameter threaded rod
6 1/2" cut washers
2 3/8" locking washers
2 3/8" cap nuts

SUGGESTED TOOLS

Layout tools
Claw hammer
Circular saw with rip fence
Jigsaw with medium-toothed blade
Rasps
3/8" drill
1/2" and 1" bradpoint bits
1/16" twist-drill bit
Pilot bits for 1", 1-1/4", and 1-5/8" deck screws
Router with chamfer bit adjusted for 3/16" cut
Pad sander

CUT LIST

1 Front • 3/4" x 7-1/4" x 12"
2 Sides • 3/4" x 6-7/8" x 18"
2 Long side trims • 3/4" x 1-11/16" x 29-7/8"
2 Short side trims • 3/4" x 1-11/16" x 13-1/4"
2 Side angle trims • 3/4" x 1-11/16" x 5-3/4"
2 Leg trims • 3/4" x 1-11/16" x 12"
1 End cap • 3/4" x 1-1/4" x 12"
2 Side bottom supports • 1/2" x 3/4" x 14-11/16"
1 Rear bottom support • 1/2" x 3/4" x 10-15/16"
1 Front bottom support • 1/2" x 7/8" x 10-15/16"
2 Axle supports • 3/4" x 4" x 4-1/2"
1 Cross brace • 3/4" x 3" x 13-1/2"
1 Bottom • 1/2" x 12" x 14-15/16" plywood
1 Handle • 1" x 14-1/4" dowel

TIPS

- *Pressure-treated lumber is recommended for this outdoor project.*

- *The trim pieces can be cut to width by ripping along the center of 3-1/2"-wide stock.*

- *Some pieces have angle cuts on one or both ends; the dimensions in the Cut List reflect the longest length or widest width of each piece before it's cut to size.*

- *Because steel-hubbed wheels vary in hub length, refer to "Steel Wheels and Axles" (page 39) before cutting the threaded rod and the tubing to final length. The lengths in the Cut List are examples that fit the 1-3/8" hub length of the wheels used in the project built for this book.*

GARDEN CART

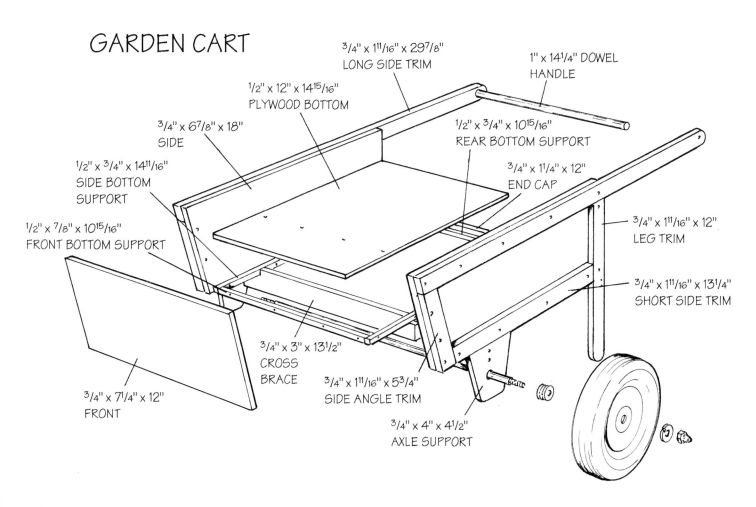

3/4" x 1^{11}/16" x 29^{7}/8"
LONG SIDE TRIM

1/2" x 12" x 14^{15}/16"
PLYWOOD BOTTOM

1" x 14^{1}/4" DOWEL
HANDLE

3/4" x 6^{7}/8" x 18"
SIDE

1/2" x 3/4" x 10^{15}/16"
REAR BOTTOM SUPPORT

1/2" x 3/4" x 14^{11}/16"
SIDE BOTTOM
SUPPORT

3/4" x 1^{1}/4" x 12"
END CAP

3/4" x 1^{11}/16" x 12"
LEG TRIM

1/2" x 7/8" x 10^{15}/16"
FRONT BOTTOM SUPPORT

3/4" x 1^{11}/16" x 13^{1}/4"
SHORT SIDE TRIM

3/4" x 3" x 13^{1}/2"
CROSS
BRACE

3/4" x 7^{1}/4" x 12"
FRONT

3/4" x 1^{11}/16" x 5^{3}/4"
SIDE ANGLE TRIM

3/4" x 4" x 4^{1}/2"
AXLE SUPPORT

INSTRUCTIONS

1. Rip the side-piece stock to 6-7/8" in width. Then use your square and adjustable protractor to lay out two side pieces. Each has one square end and one end angled at 15 degrees; the longest edge of each is 18". Cut the two side pieces to size with your circular saw.

2. Mark and cut the front piece to length from 7-1/4" stock. Then lay out and cut parallel, 15-degree bevels on each edge; the width of the finished piece should be 7".

3. On the outer face of each side piece, 3/8" from the angled end, mark and bore a line of four equally-spaced pilot holes for 1-1/4" deck screws.

4. Using eight 1-1/4" deck screws, attach the two side pieces to the ends of the front piece.

5. Lay out the remaining wooden parts, referring to the "Cut List" and to the Axle Support/Brace Layout diagram. Cut the pieces to size with your circular saw and, when making the cuts in the dowel handle and the notches in the cross brace, with your back-saw. The following parts receive one or more angled or beveled 15-degree cuts: the front end of the bottom piece; the long-side, short-side, and side-angle trim pieces; the side bottom supports; and the front bottom support.

6. Use your compass to lay out a 27/32" radius on one end of each leg trim and on the 90-degree end of each long side trim. Cut the radii with your jigsaw.

7. Temporarily clamp the parts together, aligning them exactly. Mark the locations for chamfering and, after taking the assembly apart, use your router to chamfer all arrises that will not meet others once the project is assembled.

8. Position the end cap between the two side pieces so that its outer face is flush with the ends of the side pieces. To attach it, use two pilot-bored 1-1/4" deck screws driven through each side and into an end of the cap.

9. In the 3/4" faces of the four bottom supports, bore pilot holes for 1" deck screws, spacing them 1-1/2" apart. Use 1" deck screws to attach the side supports to the inner faces of the side pieces, aligning all bottom edges. Attach the front and rear bottom supports to the inside faces of the front piece and end cap, respectively.

10. Place the plywood bottom on the supports and bore pilot holes for 1" deck screws around its perimeter, approximately 2-1/2" apart and 5/16" from the edges and ends. (Locate these holes so that they won't interfere with the screws installed in Step 9.) Attach the bottom with 1" deck screws.

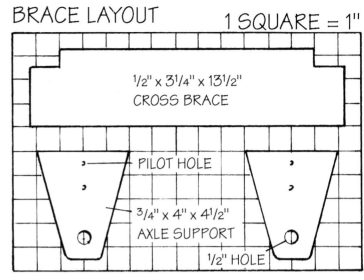

BRACE LAYOUT   1 SQUARE = 1"

1/2" x 3 1/4" x 13 1/2"
CROSS BRACE

PILOT HOLE

3/4" x 4" x 4 1/2"
AXLE SUPPORT

1/2" HOLE

AXLE SUPPORT/

11. Lay out and bore a row of eight pilot holes for 1-1/4" deck screws through the end cap and into the edge of the bottom. Begin 3/4" from either end of the end cap and space the holes 1-1/2" apart and 1/4" from the end cap's upper edge. (Avoid hitting the screws installed in Step 10.) Then install the 1-1/4" deck screws.

12. Bore and install two more 1-1/4" deck screws in the end cap, locating each one 1/4" from each end and 3/8" from the bottom edge; these screws will enter the side bottom supports.

13. On the inside face of each long side trim, centered across its width and 7/8" from the rounded end, lay out and bore a 1"-wide, 3/8"-deep hole for the handle.

14. Position the other trim pieces on the boxlike assembly. Then mark and bore the pilot holes required to attach them with 1-1/4" deck screws, spacing these holes approximately 3-1/2" apart. Through the outside face of each long side trim, also bore a pilot hole for a 1-5/8" deck screw, centering it over the 1" hole bored previously. Adjust the length of all trim pieces as necessary.

15. Bore a 1/16" pilot hole, 1-1/8" deep, into the center of each end of the dowel handle. (Use your center finder when marking the ends.)

16. Using glue and 1-1/4" deck screws, attach the trim pieces to one side of the assembly.

WHEEL/AXLE DETAIL

3/4" x 4" x 4¹/₂"
AXLE SUPPORT

3/4" x 3¹/₄" x 13¹/₂"
CROSS BRACE

8" x 1.75
RUBBER-TIRED
WHEEL

1⁵/₈" DECK
SCREW

3/8" LOCK WASHER

18¹/₂" x ¹/₂" O.D. TUBING

3/8" x 19"
THREADED ROD

1⁷/₈"

3/8" CAP NUT

STACKED ¹/₂" CUT
WASHER PROVIDE
TIRE CLEARANCE

ALLOW ¹/₁₆" SPACE
BETWEEN HUB AND
END OF TUBE/LOCK WASHER

17. Using a 1-5/8" deck screw, install the handle in the 1" hole in the attached long side trim. Then attach the remaining trim pieces to the opposite side of the assembly. Don't forget to insert a deck screw into the other end of the handle.

18. In the face of each axle support, bore two pilot holes for 1-5/8" deck screws, 1/2" and 1-1/2" from the wide end and centered across the support's width. Also bore a centered 1/2"-diameter axle through-hole, 1-7/8" from the narrow end.

19. Using two 1-5/8" deck screws at each joint, attach one face of each axle support to each end of the cross brace.

20. In the top face of the bottom piece, 12-1/4" from the end cap's outside face, bore a row of four pilot holes for 1-5/8" deck screws. Space these 2-1/2" apart and run them parallel to the front edge of the bottom piece.

21. Attach the notched edge of the cross brace to the underside of the bottom piece, using 1-5/8" deck screws driven through the pilot holes just drilled. The 1-1/4" notch should be flush with the flat end of the axle support.

22. Sand all surfaces thoroughly and remove the sanding debris.

23. Finish the cart with exterior-grade materials.

24. Refer to the "Tips" section before proceeding. Cut the 1/2" tubing and 3/8" threaded rod to length, smoothing the ends with a file. Slide the tubing through the holes in the axle supports so that it projects an equal distance beyond the outside face of each support. Slip the rod through the tubing and place the cut washers, a wheel, a locking washer, and a cap nut over one projecting end. Tighten the cap nut securely. Repeat the hardware assembly on the other end of the tubing, using two adjustable wrenches to grip the cap nuts. Your Garden Cart's finished!

GAS

OIL

Movin' On:
Specialty Vehicles, Displays, and Gear

WESTERN PONY

• • • •

Here's a delicate rocking showpiece
for your child's display shelf.

CUT LIST

1 Body • 1/4" x 2-7/8" x 6-5/8"
2 Front sides • 1/4" x 2-3/4" x 4-1/8"
2 Rear sides • 1/4" x 2-1/4" x 3-7/8"
2 Rockers • 1/4" x 1-15/16" x 7-5/8"
2 Braces • 1/4" x 3/8" x 1-1/2"

HARDWARE AND SUPPLIES

8 No. 18 x 5/8" brads
4 No. 18 x 7/8" brads

SUGGESTED TOOLS

Layout tools
Fretsaw
Rasps
Claw hammer
3/8" drill
1/32" twist-drill bit

TIPS

• *This delicate project is too fragile for play and
should be displayed out of reach of little fingers.*

• *The wooden parts are balsa, a crafts material available at craft stores.*

• *The thin, fine-toothed blade of the fretsaw is ideal
for cutting balsa wood. If you don't have access to
this tool, use a coping saw instead.*

INSTRUCTIONS

1. Enlarge the cutting patterns for the body, two front
sides, two rear sides, and two rockers. Then transfer
them to your 1/4" stock, along with the boring locations on the rockers and the brace locations on the
rockers' inside faces.

2. With your fretsaw, cut the curved shapes out, using
gentle pressure and adequate support. Cut the
braces, which aren't curved, with a utility knife.

3. Use fine-toothed rasps and sandpaper to roughly
shape the parts to your liking, taking care not to
sand arrises that will be joined during assembly.
Remove the sanding debris.

WESTERN PONY

$1/4" \times 2^7/8" \times 6^5/8"$
BODY

$1/4" \times 2^3/4" \times 4^1/8"$
FRONT SIDE

$1/4" \times 2^1/4" \times 3^7/8"$
REAR SIDE

$1/4" \times 1^{15}/16" \times 7^5/8"$
ROCKER

$1/4" \times 3/8" \times 1^1/2"$
BRACE

NO. 18 $\times$ $7/8"$
BRAD

4. Glue and clamp the side pieces to the body piece. Before the glue sets up, check that all four side pieces are aligned by setting the figure on a flat surface such as a tabletop. The hooves should all rest squarely on the surface, and their tips should be exactly 5-5/8" apart from front to back. If the parts are off even slightly, realign them as necessary.

5. Using your 1/32" bit, bore the four pilot holes in the outer face of each rocker. Marking the bit with tape will prevent you from drilling too deeply.

6. Apply a bit of glue to one end of each brace, position the braces on the inside face of a rocker, and use a brad setter or claw hammer to secure each one with No. 18 x 5/8" brads driven through the pilot holes. Light pressure is essential! Using the same method, attach the second rocker in place.

7. Using rasps and sandpaper, complete the shaping of the figure.

8. Secure the figure upside down. Set the rocker assembly onto the figure's hooves so that the braces are exactly aligned with the tips of the hooves and the hooves are centered across the length of the braces. Bore two 1/32" pilot holes, 7/8" deep, through the edge of each brace and into the hooves, aiming the bit carefully to pierce the center of each hoof and leg.

9. Secure the figure in place by installing four No. 18 x 7/8" brads in the pilot holes.

10. Set the assembled pony on a flat surface. If it doesn't rest with its back parallel to the surface, adjust its position by using one or more No. 6 x 1" deck screws as counterbalances. Insert these screws into pilot-bored holes (use a 1/16" bit) in the bottom edge of the body, concealing them between the legs and placing them towards the end of the figure that is tilted highest.

11. Remove every speck of dust from the assembly. After priming, paint the Western Pony as you imagine it might look in the wild country. Your child will love it!

galloping ghosts

Toy horses that move by means of wheels, rockers, or other mechanisms have been centerpieces in children's nurseries for centuries; the best examples exhibit a larger-than-life quality that kids love. The technical and creative ingenuity evident in the antique ponies shown here should inspire any builder.

This handsome, time-worn hobby horse is typical of finely detailed riding toys manufactured in England around the turn of the century. The gentle swaying motion of this rod-supported heirloom toy is still silky smooth, and its  well-worn velvet and leather trappings signify a thousand happy hours of youthful horsemanship. Its horsehair mane and tail complete the illusion of a stamping, snorting steed. Similar horse figures from the same period are also found on rockers or suspended from springs, producing altogether different but equally charming movements.

Courtesy of King-Thomasson Antiques, Inc.,
Asheville, North Carolina.

Proud toddlers of the Victorian era pulled wheeled horses just like the one shown here. Note that its string was once attached in a similar fashion to the strings on the pull toys in this book. Though the horse depicted has seen a hard life, its original  beauty can be glimpsed in the powerfully sculpted forms of its body and in its prancing gait.

The key to making a figure toy come alive is to slightly exaggerate its natural shape, creating muscular rhythms that fairly shout movement. Let your imagination fly free and gift your kids with a thrilling ride they'll never forget.

PRIZEWINNER
● ● ● ●

This old-timey "carved" sheep figure on its wheeled base is actually shaped with rasps.

CUT LIST

1 Base • 3/4" x 3-1/2" x 10"
4 Wheels (Type A) • 3/4" x 1"-diameter
2 Axles • 1/4" x 3-1/2" dowel
1 Body center • 3/4" x 4" x 8-3/8"
2 Body sides • 3/4" x 6-13/16" x 8-3/8"

HARDWARE AND SUPPLIES

4 1-1/4" deck screws
4 No. 18 x 5/8" brads
4 Size 112 small screw eyes

SUGGESTED TOOLS

Layout tools
Backsaw and miter box
Circular saw
Jigsaw with scrolling blade
Rasps
Claw hammer
No. 2 Phillips screwdriver
3/8" drill
1/16", 1/8", and 3/32" twist-drill bits
Countersink bit
1" hole saw with 1/4" guide bit
Router with chamfer bit adjusted for 3/16" cut
Pad sander

INSTRUCTIONS

1. Lay out and cut the three body pieces to the sizes specified in the "Cut List." Then glue them together in sandwich fashion, with one 8-3/8" edge and both ends of each aligned. Clamp the assembly together with approximately one dozen clamps, spaced to assure a tightly glued assembly. Set the assembly aside to dry thoroughly.

2. Cut the base to size and the axles to length. Then cut the four Type A wheels (see page 37), using a 1" hole saw fitted with a 1/4" guide bit.

3. Chamfer all arrises on the base, using your router fitted with a chamfer bit adjusted for 3/16".

4. On the bottom face of the base, mark locations for the screw eyes. Each mark should be approximately 1" from an end and 7/8" from an edge.

5. Bore a 3/32" hole, 1/2" deep, at each location.

6. Install a screw eye in each hole, turning it until the center of the eye is approximately 9/16" from the base. Align the eyes' openings with the edges of the base.

7. Using your flat rasp and sandpaper, round the ends of the axles. Slip the axles through the paired screw eyes and position the wheels on the axles so that 1/8" of axle protrudes from the outside face of each wheel. Secure the wheels with brads (see page 39).

8. Remove the clamps from the body assembly and scrape away any glue that protrudes. Enlarge the cutting pattern and transfer it to one side of the assembly.

9. Using your jigsaw and scrolling blade, cut through the sandwich's thickness along the pattern lines. Then secure the figure with the leg shapes turned upwards and cut out the rough shapes of the legs with your coping saw. Turn the figure so that the head and back face upwards and shape them with your coping saw as well. Use caution at all times to avoid splitting the thinner parts of the figure!

10. Using flat, round, and half-round rasps, soften the squared arrises left from the saws, approximating the bone, muscle, and wool of the animal (see photo). Especially light strokes are essential when you shape the delicate legs. To make a small notch for the mouth at the bottom of the muzzle, use a narrow edge of your half-round rasp.

11. Fill any cracks or other problem areas with wood filler and let the filler dry. Then sand the figure carefully, turning it this way and that in the light to be certain that no tool marks remain.

TIPS

- *While the model for this project was a Columbian breed sheep, any favorite animal can be fashioned using the methods described in the instructions.*

- *You'll need about one dozen clamps to glue up the body assembly; each should have a throat opening of at least 2-5/16".*

- *The liner brush mentioned in Step 19 is a specialty brush with a very thin, elongated tip. Ask for it at a hobby shop or paint-supply store.*

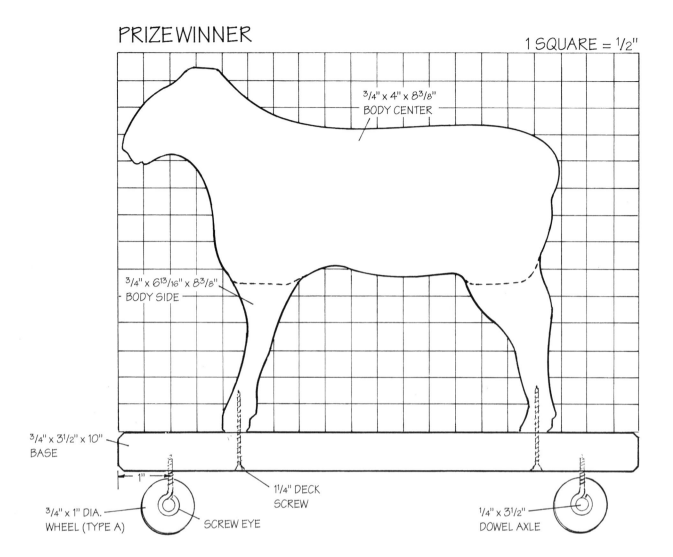

PRIZEWINNER

1 SQUARE = 1/2"

3/4" x 4" x 8 3/8"
BODY CENTER

3/4" x 6 13/16" x 8 3/8"
BODY SIDE

3/4" x 3 1/2" x 10"
BASE

1"

1 1/4" DECK
SCREW

3/4" x 1" DIA.
WHEEL (TYPE A)

SCREW EYE

1/4" x 3 1/2"
DOWEL AXLE

12. Center the figure on the top face of the base, between its edges and ends. Use your pencil to trace each hoof shape onto the base and then bore four 1/8" holes through the face, locating each hole towards the back portion of each hoof so that the mounting screws will be directed into the thickest parts of the hooves.

13. Turn the base over and, at each hole, make a countersink for a deck screw.

14. Set the sheep figure back on the base, aligning the hooves and holes carefully.

15. With a 1/16" bit, bore a 1/2"-deep hole through each counterbore into the center of each hoof. (The boring depth is 1-1/4" from the bottom face of the base.)

16. To secure the figure to the base, drive 1-1/4" deck screws through the counterbored holes.

17. Prime the assembly and let it dry thoroughly. Then paint the base, wheels, and axles. In the project shown, the base and axles were painted with bright colors to contrast with the more subdued colors of the figure and wheels.

18. To paint the figure, first apply a couple of base coats of off-white latex enamel paint. Off-white is made by mixing a few drops of brown or umber paint together with a larger volume of white paint. (Avoid mixing paints with differing ingredients.)

19. Paint the figure's eyes, ears, hooves, wool, and other details with a liner brush, using warm gray and black latex enamel paints. (Add a prize ribbon, if you like, in bright colors.) You can either paint simplified details or work towards a more realistic appearance by shading the various parts to further define the animal's shape. Either way, your youngster will love you for your efforts!

ROPE WALKER
• • • •

The simple mechanics of this balancing acrobat create a mystifying piece for a shelf in your child's room.

CUT LIST

1 Rope walker • 1/4" x 3" x 4-1/2"
1 Crowd • 1/4" x 3-1/2" x 9"
1 Base • 1/4" x 3-1/2" x 12"
2 Posts • 3/8" x 7-1/2" dowel
2 Axle supports • 3/4" x 1-1/4" x 1-3/4"
2 Axles • 1/4" x 3-5/8" dowel
4 Wheels (Type A) • 3/4" x 1-3/8"-diameter

HARDWARE AND SUPPLIES

4 3/4" deck screws
8 No. 17 x 3/4" brads
1 14" length of 12-gauge copper wire
1 10" length of No. 2 braided picture wire
2 3/4 oz. fishing weights
2 Size 7 split-shot fishing weights
Wood filler

SUGGESTED TOOLS

Layout tools
Backsaw and miter box
Circular saw
Coping saw
Jigsaw with scrolling blade
Rasps
Claw hammer
No. 2 Phillips screwdriver
3/8" drill
3/8" bradpoint bit
3/64" and 3/32" twist-drill bits
Pilot bit for 3/4" deck screws
1-3/8" hole saw with 1/4" guide bit
Pad sander
Wire-cutting and needle-nose pliers

TIPS

- *Purchase the recommended fishing weights at a fishing-supply store.*
- *If you don't have 1/4"-thick solid wood stock on hand, ask for some small pieces at a local cabinet shop. Plywood is not recommended for this project.*
- *You'll find copper wire of the right size in 12-gauge electrical wire, which contains a copper-wire core; just strip off the plastic coating.*

ROPE WALKER

1 SQUARE = 1/2"

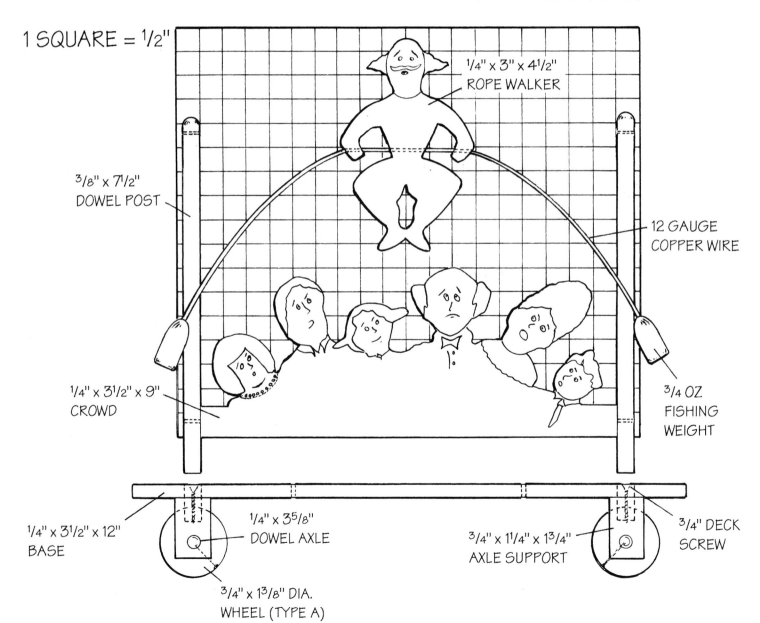

1/4" x 3" x 4 1/2" ROPE WALKER

3/8" x 7 1/2" DOWEL POST

12 GAUGE COPPER WIRE

1/4" x 3 1/2" x 9" CROWD

3/4 OZ FISHING WEIGHT

1/4" x 3 1/2" x 12" BASE

1/4" x 3 5/8" DOWEL AXLE

3/4" x 1 1/4" x 1 3/4" AXLE SUPPORT

3/4" DECK SCREW

3/4" x 1 3/8" DIA. WHEEL (TYPE A)

INSTRUCTIONS

1. Enlarge the walker and crowd patterns and transfer them (including the hole locations) onto 1/4" stock. Carefully cut out the two shapes with your jigsaw and scrolling blade.

2. In the walker, carefully bore the 3/32" through-hole for the copper wire, centering the hole in the body's 1/4" thickness and applying as little pressure as possible to avoid splitting the thin wood. (Bore one hand and the body from one side; then switch sides to bore the second hand.)

3. Secure the walker upside down. Using your coping saw, make a 1/4"-deep cut across the figure's feet, aligning it to run at an angle of approximately 22-1/2 degrees to the length of the feet (see Rope Walker Detail). Then, with your backsaw, widen the cut slightly to create a groove that is 1/4" deep and the width of the saw's teeth.

ROPE WALKER DETAIL 1/4" DEEP GROOVE

22 1/2°

4. Using your flat and round rasps, smooth both the angled cut you just made and the groove that runs perpendicular to and between the two feet.

5. Lay out and cut to size the base, axle supports, axles, and the four 1-3/8"-diameter Type A wheels (see page 37).

6. Secure an axle support on end and mark a point 3/8" from an edge and 3/8" from a face. At that point, carefully bore a 9/32" hole straight through the length of the piece. Repeat with the second axle support.

7. In the upper face of the base, lay out and bore two pairs of pilot holes for 3/4" deck screws. Locate each hole 1-5/16" from an end and 1-1/4" from an edge; countersink each hole slightly.

8. Fasten the edge of the each axle support to the bottom of the base, centering each one across the width of the base and attaching it with 3/4" deck screws inserted through the predrilled holes. Patch the holes with wood filler.

9. Lay out and bore two 3/8" holes, 3/4" deep, into the base's top face. Locate each hole 1-5/16" from an end and 1-3/4" from an edge.

10. Measure and cut the two posts to length and use your flat rasp to round one end of each.

11. Glue the flat ends of the posts into the two post holes.

12. Lay out and bore two 3/64" holes through the width of each post. Locate the first hole 3/8" from the rounded top and the second 3/8" above the top of the base; make sure that all holes are bored in the same direction. Also bore two 3/64" holes through the base, locating each hole 3-1/2" from an end and 1-3/4" from an edge.

13. Carefully sand all parts, paying particular attention to the walker and crowd pieces and rounding the ends of the axles well. After removing all sanding debris, prime all parts with latex enamel primer. When the primer has dried, sand lightly, remove any dust, and paint the parts with latex enamel paints. Let all parts dry thoroughly.

14. Center the crowd between the two posts and secure it with four brads driven through the holes in the posts and base.

15. Assemble the wheels on the axles and axle supports, allowing the axle ends to extend 1/8" beyond the wheels' outside faces. Secure the wheels with brads (see page 39). Repaint any wheel parts that were scratched during assembly.

16. To form a tightrope, slip the picture wire through the upper holes in the posts and secure the ends by clamping a split shot fishing weight onto each one.

17. Slide the copper wire through the hole in the walker, centering the body along its length. Avoid using force, as the walker is delicate! With a 3/32" twist-drill bit, carefully bore a hole through each brass weight. Slip one end of the wire through each hole. To secure the weights in place, use pliers to bend the wire ends.

18. Now for the fun part! Gently form an arc by bending the copper wire downward beyond the walker's feet. Set the walker near the center of the tightrope, placing the angled slot between its feet onto the rope. To balance the walker in this position, adjust the weights laterally and vertically by bending the wire. To balance the walker perpendicular to the length of the base, fit the 90-degree groove between his feet onto the tightrope and adjust the weights as necessary. The first arrangement is ideal for a narrow shelf, while the latter is perfect for a table or desk.

GAS PUMP

· · · ·

*This pump comes complete with a gas filler
and crank. Add the optional Squeegee
and Oilcan projects if you like
and let the fun begin!*

CUT LIST

- 2 Front and back panels • 3/4" x 14" x 35-1/2"
- 2 Uprights • 3-1/2" x 3-1/2" x 35-1/2"
- 1 Window sign • 2-1/2" x 2-1/2" x 7"
- 1 Short crank • 1" x 2" dowel
- 1 Long crank • 1" x 5-1/2" dowel
- 1 Crank • 3/4" x 2" x 5"
- 1 Crank handle • 1" x 2-1/2"
- 2 Window supports • 1-1/2" x 3-1/2" x 8"
- 1 Cap • 3/4" x 3-1/2" x 15"
- 1 Top sign • 3/4" x 3-1/2" x 8"
- 2 Sign supports • 3/8" x 2" dowel
- 1 Base • 1-1/2" x 9-1/2" x 19"
- 1 Hose grip • 1-1/2" x 1-1/2" x 3-1/2"
- 1 Filler handle • 1-1/2" x 5-1/2" x 6"
- 1 Filler holder • 1-1/2" x 1-1/2" x 6"
- 1 Spout • 3/4" x 5" dowel

HARDWARE AND SUPPLIES

- 1 1-1/4" deck screw
- 1 lb. 1-1/2" deck screws
- 2 2" deck screws
- 12 2-1/2" deck screws
- 1 48" length of 7/8" garden hose

SUGGESTED TOOLS

Layout tools
Backsaw and miter box
Circular saw
Jigsaw with plywood blade
Block plane
Rasps
No. 2 Phillips screwdriver
3/8" drill
3/8", 7/8", and 1" bradpoint bits
Pilot bits for 1-1/4", 1-1/2", 2",
    and 2-1/2" deck screws
Router with 3/8" rounding-over bit
Pad sander

TIPS

- *Keep track of the parts by labeling them with a pencil as soon as they're cut.*

- *Any garden hose with a diameter smaller than 1" is acceptable, but you'll need a bradpoint bit of a similar diameter. Because the hose is flexible, its end can often be coaxed into a hole that isn't exactly the same size.*

- *Although pilot-hole boring is not mentioned in these instructions, pilot holes of a size identical to the screws being used should be bored in every case.*

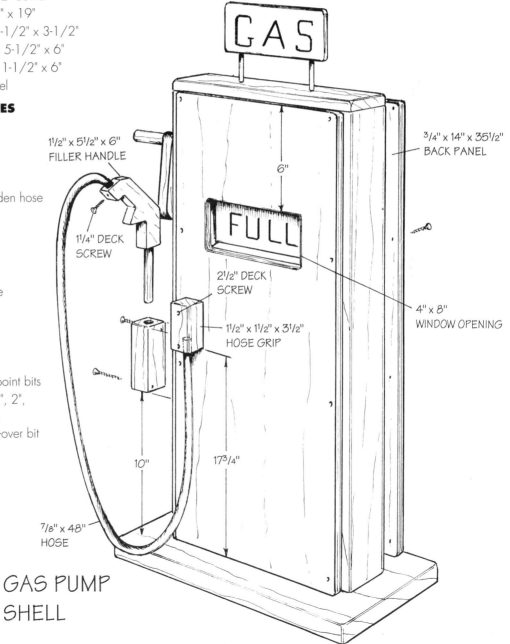

1½" x 5½" x 6"
FILLER HANDLE

1¼" DECK SCREW

2½" DECK SCREW

3/4" x 14" x 35½"
BACK PANEL

6"

4" x 8"
WINDOW OPENING

1½" x 1½" x 3½"
HOSE GRIP

10"

17³/₄"

7/8" x 48"
HOSE

GAS PUMP SHELL

INSTRUCTIONS

1. Begin by laying out and cutting the various parts to length, ripping any pieces to width and thickness as necessary. Use a circular saw on the dimension lumber and a backsaw on the smaller dowel parts.

2. Set the plywood front panel with its best face down and lay out the centered 4" x 8" window opening (see Gas Pump Shell diagram). The top of the opening should be 6" below the panel's top end and each side should be 3" from an edge.

3. Start the window cutout by boring a 3/8" hole in each inside corner of the layout. Then cut out the rectangle with your jigsaw.

4. Place one upright face up on some scrap wood. Lay out a mark 8" from one end and centered on one face. Then, at this mark, bore a 1"-diameter through-hole for the long crank dowel.

5. Repeat Step 4 with the second upright, but this time bore the 1" hole only 1-1/2" deep. This hole will accommodate the short crank dowel.

6. Mount the cap to span the two uprights, aligning its ends flush with the uprights' outer edges. Secure the cap at each end with a pair of equally spaced 1-1/2" deck screws located 1" from the end.

7. Position the front and back panels on the uprights, allowing 1/2" of upright to protrude on each side and aligning the bored portions of the uprights with the window opening (see Gas Pump Shell diagram). Secure the panels in place with 1-1/2" deck screws, spaced approximately 5" apart and located 1-1/4" from the long edge of each panel.

8. Position the two window supports in the window opening so that they're "sandwiched" between the front and back panels and face each other across the opening (see Gas Pump Frame diagram). The ends of the supports butt the inner faces of the uprights, and their inner faces align with the long edges of the window opening. Secure the supports with twelve 1-1/2" deck screws, driving three equally spaced screws through the plywood into each support edge.

9. With your router and rounding-over bit, round the arrises of the window opening, the uprights, and the cap. Also round the upper arrises of the base piece.

10. Turn the assembly upside down and center the base piece on it. Then drive two square groups of four 2-1/2" deck screws through the base and into the ends of the uprights.

GAS PUMP FRAME

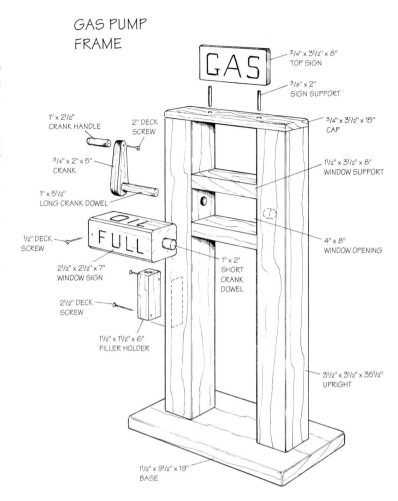

11. Using your block plane, chamfer the four long arrises of the window sign. Secure the window sign with one end facing up and bore a centered 1" hole, 5/8" deep. Repeat to bore an identical hole in the opposite end.

12. Lay out the crank (see Crank Detail) and use your jigsaw to cut it out. Then bore a 1"-diameter hole through the face so that the hole's center is 1" from the larger of the two radiused ends.

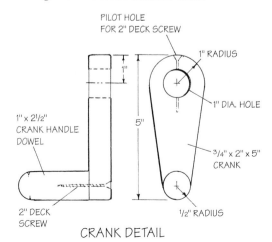

CRANK DETAIL

13. Use 2" deck screws to fasten the crank handle and long crank to the crank (see Crank Detail and Gas Pump Frame diagram).

14. Shape the crank handle's end with a half-round rasp so that it will feel comfortable in a child's hand. Then sand the window sign and crank parts carefully.

15. Glue the short crank dowel into the hole in one end of the window sign (see Gas Pump Frame diagram). Slip the sign into the window opening so that the dowel's end fits into the 1-1/2"-deep hole in the support. If the fit is tight, shape the dowel with sandpaper until it slides easily into the hole.

16. Hold the sign in the opening and slide the crank assembly's long crank through the 1" hole in the other upright and into the hole in the sign. If the dowel doesn't slide smoothly into the hole in the upright, use a round rasp to enlarge the hole. Glue the long crank's end into the hole in the window sign and let the glue joint dry thoroughly.

17. Further secure the two dowel ends in the sign by driving two 1-1/2" deck screws through one face of the sign, each 1/4" from an end and centered between the arrises.

18. Round the arrises of the top sign with your router and 3/8" rounding-over bit. Then bore a pair of 3/8" holes, spaced 6" apart, into the face of the cap; bore another pair into the sign's bottom edge. To mount the top sign, glue two 3/8" x 2" dowels into the paired holes.

19. Secure the filler holder with one end facing up and, in the center of its top end, bore a 1" hole, 4-1/2" deep (see Filler/Holder Detail). Mount the holder to the upright, centering it on the upright's face and locating its bottom end 10" above the base (see Gas Pump Shell diagram). Drive two 2-1/2" deck screws through its face, locating these screws on a diagonal so that they don't enter the 4-1/2"-deep hole.

20. Using a drill bit of the same diameter as your hose, bore a centered 1-1/2"-deep hole in one end of the hose grip. Insert one end of the hose into the hole. Then position the grip vertically on the front panel, 3-3/4" from the panel's edge and 17-3/4" from the base; the hose should extend from its bottom end (see Gas Pump Shell diagram). Fasten the grip in place with two 2-1/2" screws, centered along the hose grip's length and spaced 2-1/2" apart. (The bottom screw will secure one end of the hose.)

21. Using your jigsaw, cut out the filler handle (see Filler/Holder Detail). Bore a 3/4" hole for the spout, 1" deep and centered in the end. Also bore a 3/4"-deep hole centered in the opposite end, sizing its diameter to that of the hose.

22. Glue the spout into the 3/4" hole. Fasten the hose inside the other hole by driving a 1-1/4" deck screw through the handle's edge, locating it 3/8" from the end so that the screw will pierce the hose.

23. Carefully sand all parts of the Gas Pump, paying particular attention to those that will be handled repeatedly.

24. Before painting the project with latex enamel paints, prime it well with latex primer. Finish unpainted parts with an exterior-grade water-based varnish. The window sign in the Gas Pump pictured features one word on each face of the rotating sign: FULL, EMPTY, OIL, and CLEAN.

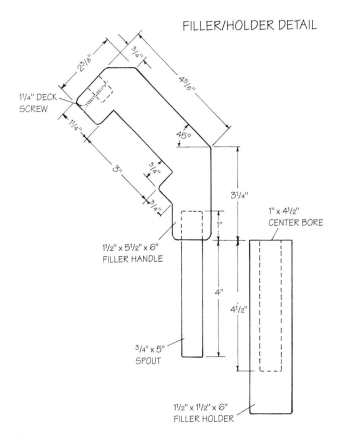

FILLER/HOLDER DETAIL

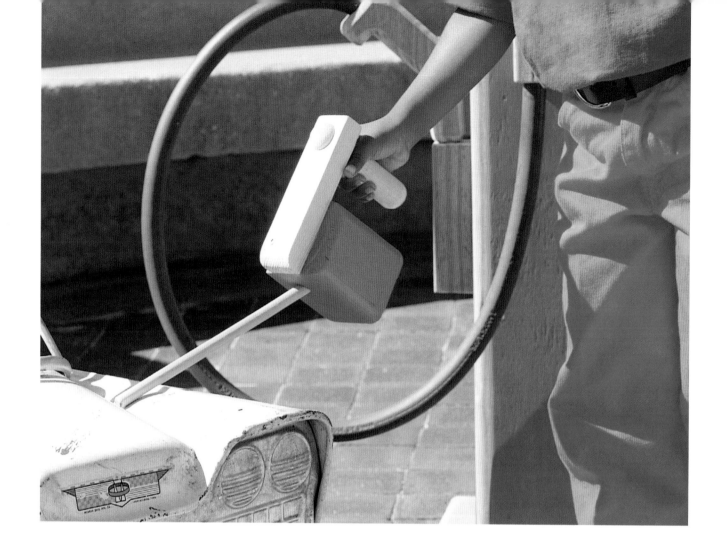

OILCAN

• • • •

*Although it was designed to go with
the Gas Pump project, this simple wooden toy
can just as easily be enjoyed by itself.*

CUT LIST

1 Can • 2-1/2" x 2-1/2" x 3-1/2"
1 Handle support • 3/4" x 1-1/2" x 5-1/2"
1 Handle • 1" x 4-1/2" dowel
1 Spout • 3/8" x 10" dowel
1 Holder • 1-1/2" x 3-1/2" x 4"
1 Stem • 1" x 1-3/4" dowel

HARDWARE AND SUPPLIES

3 1-1/2" deck screws
2 2-1/2" deck screws

SUGGESTED TOOLS

Layout tools
Backsaw and miter box
Circular saw
Rasps
No. 2 Phillips screwdriver
3/8" drill
3/8" and 1" bradpoint bits
Pilot bits for 1-1/2" and 2-1/2" deck screws
Pad sander

OILCAN

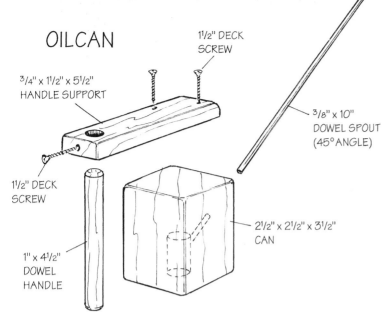

3/4" x 1½" x 5½"
HANDLE SUPPORT

1½" DECK
SCREW

1½" DECK
SCREW

1" x 4½"
DOWEL
HANDLE

3/8" x 10"
DOWEL SPOUT
(45° ANGLE)

2½" x 2½" x 3½"
CAN

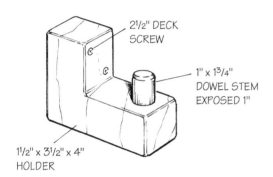

2½" DECK
SCREW

1" x 1¾"
DOWEL STEM
EXPOSED 1"

1½" x 3½" x 4"
HOLDER

INSTRUCTIONS

1. Use your circular saw to rip and cut to length the 2-1/2" x 2-1/2" x 3-1/2" can. For safety's sake, always allow plenty of extra stock when you saw small pieces like this one.

2. Bore two holes in the can: one 1" hole, 1-1/4" deep, in the center of one end; and one 3/8" hole, 1" deep, into an adjacent face. Locate the 3/8" hole in the center of the face and angle it at 45 degrees (see assembly diagram).

3. Lay out the handle support on 3/4" stock. Then rip and crosscut it to its 1-1/2" x 5-1/2" dimensions.

4. Through one face of the handle support, bore a 1" hole, 1" from an end and centered across the face.

5. Use your backsaw to cut the 1" dowel handle to 4-1/2" in length and the 3/8" dowel spout to 10" in length.

6. Use a flat rasp to round both ends of the handle, one end of the spout, and the end of the handle support that is farthest from the 1" hole.

7. Slide the handle into the hole in the handle support; 3/8" of its end should protrude above the face with the rounded arris. Secure the handle in place by centering and then driving a 1-1/2" deck screw through the end of the support and into the handle.

8. Set the can so that the end with no hole faces up. Place the handle support on top of the can so that the end farthest from the handle is flush with the face of the can that has the 3/8" hole in it. Center the handle support on the can's end as well. Secure the handle assembly by driving two 1-1/2" deck screws through the handle support's face, locating them diagonally and 1-1/4" apart.

9. Glue the square-cut end of the spout into the 3/8" hole.

10. Secure the can upside down and use your rasp to ease the arrises that are facing up and out.

11. With your circular saw, cut the holder to 4" in length. Then lay out a 1-3/4" x 3" rectangular cutout on it. To form the L-shaped holder (see assembly diagram), remove the cutout with your backsaw.

12. With the holder's 4" edge secured to your work surface, bore a 1" hole, 3/4" deep, into the 3"-long face of the cutout. Center the hole across the width of this face, 3/4" from the holder's small end.

13. Cut the 1" x 1-3/4" dowel stem to length and glue it into the 1" hole you just bored.

14. Sand all the parts well and remove the sanding debris.

15. Attach the holder to the right side of the Gas Pump, with its bottom face 12" from the bottom, by driving two 2-1/2" deck screws through the inside face of the holder's smaller "leg" (see Holder Placement diagram).

16. Test-fit the can's 1" hole onto the stem of the holder. If it doesn't fit easily, rasp or sand the stem as necessary.

17. Finish the Oilcan in any way you wish.

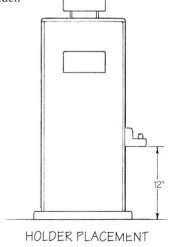

12"

HOLDER PLACEMENT

SQUEEGEE

• • • •

Kids will keep their vehicles' windshields squeaky clean with this easy-to-build project.

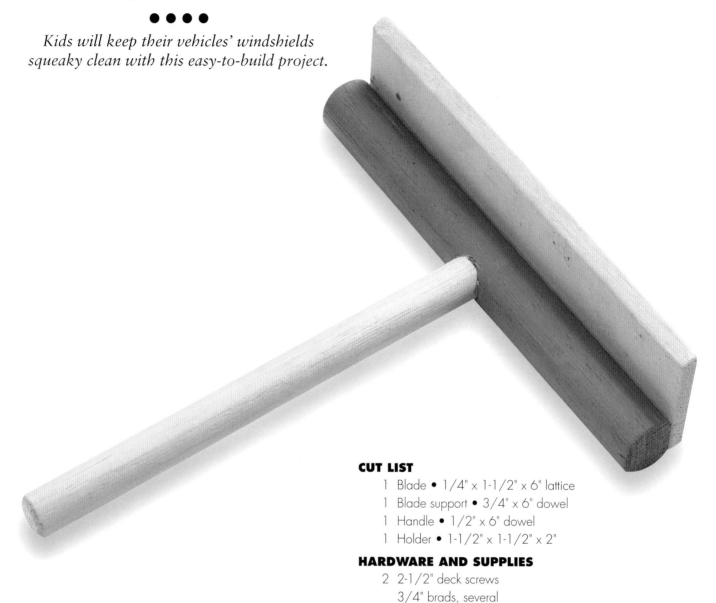

CUT LIST

1 Blade • 1/4" x 1-1/2" x 6" lattice
1 Blade support • 3/4" x 6" dowel
1 Handle • 1/2" x 6" dowel
1 Holder • 1-1/2" x 1-1/2" x 2"

HARDWARE AND SUPPLIES

2 2-1/2" deck screws
3/4" brads, several

SUGGESTED TOOLS

Layout tools
Backsaw and miter box
Circular saw
Block plane
Claw hammer
No. 2 Phillips screwdriver
3/8" drill
5/8" bradpoint bit
Pilot bit for 2-1/2" deck screws
Pad sander

INSTRUCTIONS

1. Lay out the blade, the blade support, and the handle, and cut them to length with your backsaw. Use your circular saw to cut the holder to length.

2. With your block plane, make a bevel on one edge of the blade. Then plane the length of the blade support to make a 1/2"-wide flat surface on it (see assembly diagram). Neither the bevel angle nor the width of the flat surface is critical.

3. Set the flat edge of the blade flush with one arris on the support's flat and fasten the pieces together with a little glue and several 3/4" brads.

4. Flip the assembly over and bore a 1/2" hole, 1/4"-deep, into the center of the blade support's length. Insert the dowel handle into the hole and secure it with a drop of glue.

5. Set the holder face up and bore a 5/8" hole through its face, centered 3/4" from an edge and 3/4" from an end.

6. Sand the Squeegee and holder thoroughly.

7. Position the holder on the Gas Pump project, with its upper face 6" down from the pump's top (see Squeegee Holder Placement). Secure it in place with two pilot-bored 2-1/2" deck screws driven into the end nearest the hole; locate these screws on a diagonal so that they don't pierce the 5/8" hole.

8. Finish the Squeegee in any way you wish.

SQUEEGEE

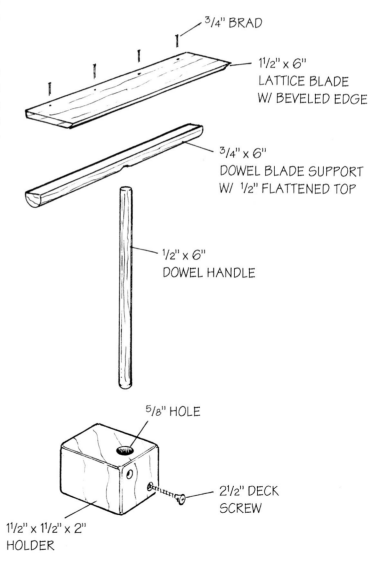

³/4" BRAD

1¹/2" x 6" LATTICE BLADE W/ BEVELED EDGE

³/4" x 6" DOWEL BLADE SUPPORT W/ ¹/2" FLATTENED TOP

¹/2" x 6" DOWEL HANDLE

5/8" HOLE

2¹/2" DECK SCREW

1¹/2" x 1¹/2" x 2" HOLDER

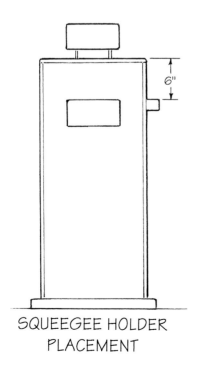

6"

SQUEEGEE HOLDER PLACEMENT

ROAD SIGNS

• • • •

Traffic signs fascinate young children, so let them choose their favorites when you make this set and encourage them to participate in basic tasks such as painting backgrounds.

CUT LIST (for four signs)

4   Standards • 1" x 23-5/8" dowel
8   Bases A and B (four pairs) • 1-1/2" x 3-1/2" x 10"
4   Signs (cut to size) • 3/8" plywood

HARDWARE AND SUPPLIES

4   2-1/2" deck screws
8   3/4" deck screws

SUGGESTED TOOLS

Layout tools
Backsaw and miter box
Circular saw
Coping saw
Chisel
Bench mallet
No. 2 Phillips screwdriver
3/8" drill
1" bradpoint bit
Pilot bits for 3/4" and 2-1/2" deck screws
Pad sander

TIP

• *Though any chisel will do, a paring chisel is perfect for cleaning up the rough corners of the cutouts on this project.*

INSTRUCTIONS

1. Use your layout tools and backsaw to lay out and cut the four dowel standards to length.

2. Secure a standard to your work surface with one end upright. With your layout tools, mark two 3-3/4" lines down opposite sides of the standard's end. Connect the two lines with a line that runs across the rounded part of the dowel (see assembly diagram).

3. Cut down the dowel's center and across its radius to remove the marked cutout.

4. Use a pilot bit to bore two holes for 3/4" screws, centered 2-3/4" apart, through the rounded back of the cutout; countersink these holes just slightly.

5. Repeat Steps 2, 3, and 4 to make cutouts and pilot holes on one end of each standard.

6. Using your layout tools and circular saw, cut the eight base pieces to length.

7. Lay out the half-lap joints on the base A and base B pieces (see detail of bases). Note that the half-lap joints on the bases A are identical in size to those on the bases B but are reversed in position. Next, secure each base piece with the edge to be cut facing up. Use your backsaw to make the vertical cuts and a coping saw to make the horizontal cuts. Use a chisel to remove any waste from the corners of each joint.

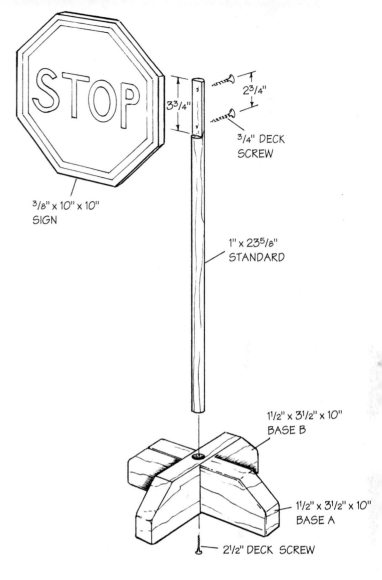

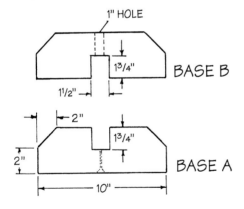

8. Test-fit the base A and B pairs and trim them as necessary.

9. Lay out the miter cuts at two adjacent corners of each base piece, making sure that the half-lap joints on all pieces are properly oriented. Secure each base piece to your work surface and make the miter cuts with a backsaw.

10. Secure one base B to your work surface, with its cutout edge facing down, and use your bradpoint bit to bore a 1" hole through the center of the top edge, right through the cutout. Repeat with the other bases B.

11. Lay out and cut the plywood sign shapes. Sizes will vary, but the stop sign shown is 10" across, and each of its angled edges is 4" long.

12. Sand all parts thoroughly.

13. Assemble the base A and B pairs by slipping the half-lap joints together. Turn each pair so that base A is on top and bore a pilot hole for a 2-1/2" deck screw through the center of the edge that faces up.

14. Flip each assembly over so that base B is on top. Then set the butt end of a standard into each 1" hole. Fasten the assemblies to the standards by driving a 2-1/2" deck screw through the pilot hole in each base A.

15. Using countersunk 3/4" screws, fasten the signs to the cutouts in the standards.

16. The bases and standards of the Road Signs shown were finished with exterior-grade water-based varnish; exterior latex primer and latex enamel paint were used on the sign shapes.

BIKE RACK

● ● ● ●

*Two-wheelers will really appreciate this
sturdy, weather-resistant bike rack.
The simple design makes it perfect for
involving your kids in its construction.*

CUT LIST

- 4 Ends (see Step 1) • 5/8" x 18" x 36-3/4" plywood
- 2 Braces • 1-1/2" x 3-1/2" x 11-3/4"
- 4 Stretchers • 1-1/2" x 1-1/2" x 38-1/2"
- 6 Stiles • 1-1/2" x 3-1/2" x 28"

HARDWARE AND SUPPLIES

- 1 lb. 1-1/4" deck screws
- 1 lb. 2-1/2" deck screws
  Construction adhesive

SUGGESTED TOOLS

Layout tools
Backsaw
Circular saw
Jigsaw with plywood blade
Chisel
Bench mallet
3/8" drill
Pilot bits for 1-1/4" and 2-1/2" deck screws
Router with 3/8" rounding-over bit
Pad sander

INSTRUCTIONS

1. Set the 5/8" plywood stock with its best face down and lay out four end pieces (see End Detail on page 134). Each of these is an isosceles triangles with two equal angles at its base. Cut out the four pieces with your circular saw; the rounded corners will be marked and cut in Step 3.

2. Pair the end pieces so that the worst face of each piece will be hidden once the pairs are fastened together. Apply construction adhesive to the inside face of one piece in each pair. Lightly clamp each pair together, aligning the edges carefully.

3. With a compass, scribe a 1" radius at every corner on both pairs. Then use your jigsaw to cut the radii.

4. Around the perimeter of one face of each pair, bore seventeen pilot holes for 1-1/4" screws, spacing the holes 1-1/4" from the edges and approximately 5" from one another (see assembly diagram). Then secure each pair by driving 1-1/4" deck screws into the holes.

5. Using your pad sander, smooth any uneven edges on the assembled pairs.

6. With your router and 3/8" rounding-over bit, round the arrises of each pair.

7. Cut the braces, stretchers, and stiles to the dimensions given in the "Cut List."

BIKE RACK

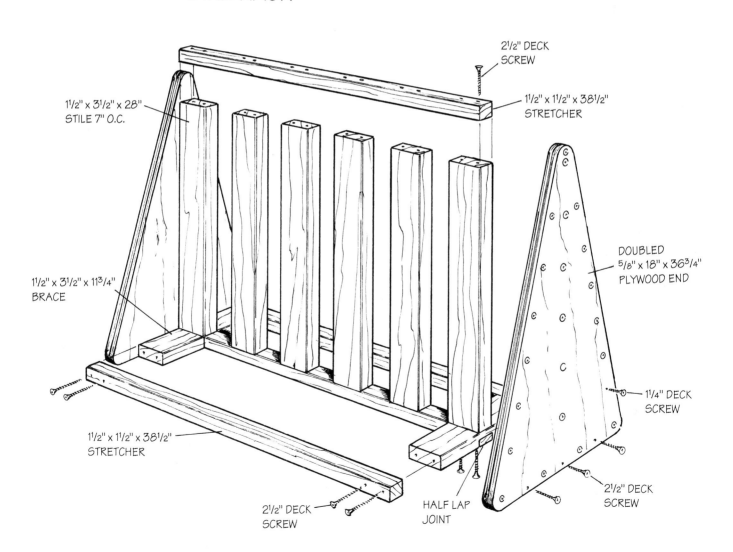

2¹⁄₂" DECK SCREW

1½" x 3½" x 28" STILE 7" O.C.

1½" x 1½" x 38½" STRETCHER

1½" x 3½" x 11¾" BRACE

DOUBLED 5/8" x 18" x 36¾" PLYWOOD END

1¼" DECK SCREW

1½" x 1½" x 38½" STRETCHER

2½" DECK SCREW

HALF LAP JOINT

2½" DECK SCREW

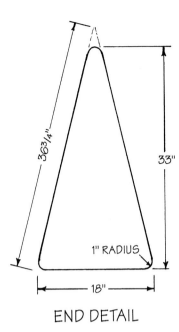

36 3/4"

33"

1" RADIUS

18"

END DETAIL

8. Secure a brace face up. Mark an open half-lap, 1-1/2" wide, 3/4" deep, and centered along the face. Set your circular-saw blade depth for 3/4", cut the square marks that define the length of the half-lap, and then use your chisel and mallet to remove the waste between the cuts. Repeat to create a half-lap in the other brace.

9. Place a stretcher face up. To mark the half-laps at the ends, first square two lines across one face, each 3-1/2" from an end. Then, on each end, square down the adjacent edges at 3/4". Use your adjustable square set for 3/4" to connect the 3/4" squared lines with the 3-1/2" lines on the face.

10. Use your backsaw to cut the 3/4"-deep lines into the face of the stretcher; a circular saw is too unstable for use on such narrow stock. Then secure the stretcher with one end up and cut into the end with your backsaw, following the marked lines on opposite faces to release the block of waste. Repeat to cut the other half-lap at the other end.

11. Test-fit the brace and stretcher joints, trimming any parts that don't fit. Fasten each joint by driving a pair of pilot-bored 1-1/4" deck screws through the brace and into the stretcher. (In the assembly diagram, these screws are hidden beneath the stiles.)

12. Secure another stretcher face up and, using your router and 3/8" rounding-over bit, round two adjacent arrises on the top face. (This stretcher will rest on top of the stiles.)

13. With your router setup, round all 28"-long arrises on the six stile pieces except for the two arrises on each outermost stile's outside edges.

14. Position the ends of the six stiles on the top stretcher's square face, centering them 7" apart and aligning the two outermost stiles flush with the stretcher's ends. Secure the top stretcher to the stiles by driving two pilot-bored 2-1/2" deck screws through it and into each stile's end.

15. Repeat Step 14 to secure the other ends of the stiles to the half-lapped stile-and-brace assembly. Make sure the half-lap cutouts in the braces face down.

16. Position the remaining two stretchers so that they span the ends of the braces. Attach them by inserting two pilot-bored 2-1/2" deck screws at each joint.

17. Align the centers of the assembled end pieces with the centers of the outermost stiles' edges. Fasten the ends in place with six pilot-bored 2-1/2" deck screws each. Use three more screws to secure each end piece to the edge of its brace.

18. Sand the assembly well, dust it off, and apply two coats of water sealer to protect the rack from the elements. Then set it out wherever your kids store their bikes.

SPOOL TRACTOR

●●●●

Your kids can help you make this simple version of an old-fashioned, slow-rolling favorite. It's powered by a rubber band.

CUT LIST

1 Spool • 1-1/4" x 2" dowel
1 Anchor • 1/8" x 3/4" dowel
1 Winder • 1/8" x 3" dowel

HARDWARE AND SUPPLIES

16 No. 17 x 5/8" brads
1 3/4" length of wax crayon
1 1/4"-wide rubber band, about 2" long

SUGGESTED TOOLS

Layout tools
Backsaw and miter box
Chisels
Claw hammer
3/8" drill
3/8" bradpoint bit
1/32" twist-drill bit
Pad sander

TIPS

- *Dowel spools from 1-1/8" to 1-3/8" in length will work well.*
- *Your materials supplier may sell the large dowel as closet rod.*

SPOOL TRACTOR

1/8" x 3"
DOWEL WINDER

1/8" X 3/4"
DOWEL ANCHOR

1/4"-WIDE
RUBBER BAND

3/4" LENGTH
OF CRAYON

1 1/4" x 2"
DOWEL SPOOL

3/16"

1/16" x 3/16" x 7/8"
NOTCH

45°

3/8" THROUGH
HOLE

NO. 17 x 5/8"
BRAD

INSTRUCTIONS

1. Lay out and cut the three dowel parts to length.

2. After using your center finder to locate the center of one end of the spool, secure the spool well and carefully bore a 3/8" hole through its center.

3. Lay out eight 1/32" equidistant pilot-hole locations around each curved edge of the spool, 3/16" from each end (see diagram).

4. Bore the holes with a 1/32" bit flagged for a 1/4" depth.

5. With your chisels and utility knife, carve a notch 3/16" wide, 1/16" deep, and 7/8" long, centered across one end of the spool. This notch should be split by the centered 3/8" hole.

6. Sand all parts lightly, rounding the small dowels' ends and easing the spool's arrises.

7. Lightly tap the brads into the pilot holes. Each one should project about 1/4".

8. Using your utility knife, cut a 3/4" length of wax crayon and round its ends. Remove any paper from the crayon.

9. Finish all wooden parts with brightly colored latex paints.

10. Slip the rubber band over the anchor and thread the other looped end through the 3/8" spool hole until the anchor rests in the notch. (Use the winder to help thread the rubber band.) Install the crayon and winder in the rubber band's opposite end, centering the crayon but offsetting the winder so that about 3/8" of its length is on one side of the rubber band and 2-5/8" is on the other.

11. Show your kids how to hold the spool in one hand and gently turn the winder several times with the other. Set the Spool Tractor on a flat surface to start its rolling action. Experiment with multiple rubber bands and the number of winding turns. Make several tractors and set up a tabletop race course. Scatter a few pencil-sized obstacles along the course and watch the slow-motion racers climb right over them!

SPACE CRUISER

· · · ·

*Every young astronaut needs wheels
for a safe touchdown! This exciting display
piece makes a great collaborative project
for you and your child.*

CUT LIST

2 Upper and lower fuselages • 1" x 2" x 9"
1 Wing • 1/4" x 7" x 9"
1 Tail • 1/4" x 2" x 3-3/4"
1 Front wheel support • 1/4" x 5/8" x 3/4"
1 Rear wheel support • 1/4" x 5/8" x 1-1/2"
4 Wheels • 1/4" x 5/8" diameter

HARDWARE AND SUPPLIES

4 No. 18 x 7/8" brads
4 No. 18 x 5/8" wire nails

SUGGESTED TOOLS

Layout tools
Backsaw and miter box
Fretsaw or coping saw
Rasps
Claw hammer
3/8" drill
1/32" and 3/32" twist-drill bits

TIPS

- *Use balsa wood, which can be purchased at most craft stores, for all wooden parts except the wheels.*
- *Note that the wheels are 5/8" in diameter, not 1/4".*
- *If 1/4"-thick balsa isn't available in widths of at least 7", fashion two matched wing halves from narrower stock and join them together along the cruiser's center line when you glue the assembly up.*

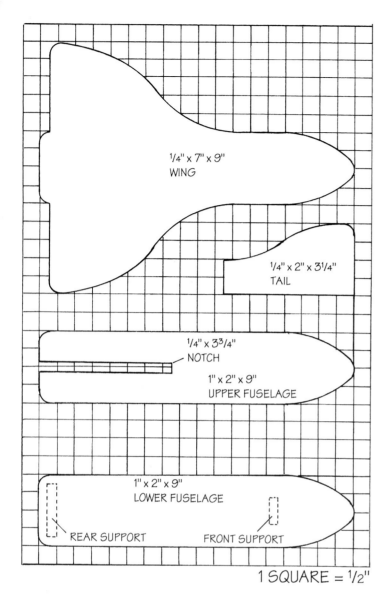

1/4" x 7" x 9"
WING

1/4" x 2" x 3¼"
TAIL

1/4" x 3¾"
NOTCH
1" x 2" x 9"
UPPER FUSELAGE

1" x 2" x 9"
LOWER FUSELAGE

REAR SUPPORT   FRONT SUPPORT

1 SQUARE = ½"

INSTRUCTIONS

1. Transfer the cutting patterns to the appropriate stock (see "Cut List"). Also transfer the locations of the front and rear supports to the lower fuselage.

2. Cut the parts out with your fretsaw; a utility knife and steel rule may work better for the straight cuts.

3. Cut out the slot in the upper fuselage.

4. Temporarily clamp the wing, fuselages, and tail together, noting that the wing is sandwiched between the fuselage pieces. Then mark the portions of the wing and tail where the fuselage pieces will overlap their surfaces after gluing. Using the photo as a guide, rasp the overall contours of the parts. Take care not to remove any wood where pieces will be joined together. Lightly sand all surfaces except the 1/4" support edges that will be glued to the fuselage.

5. Glue together the fuselage parts, wing, and tail, aligning all parts carefully and using very light clamping pressure.

6. To make the wheels, mark four 1/4" lengths of 5/8" dowel and cut them to size with your backsaw and miter box. Sand the wheels lightly after cutting.

7. In the bottom 1/4"-wide edge of each wheel support, carefully mark and bore two 1/32" pilot holes, 1/2" in from each end and offset so that the 7/8" brads placed in them won't meet the 5/8" wire nails that serve as axles for the wheels. (Note that this offset is not visible in the diagram.) Also bore a centered 3/32" pilot hole in each wheel; the wheels will spin on the 5/8" wire nails that are inserted in these holes.

8. Sand the fuselage assembly to final shape.

9. Using glue and 7/8" brads, fasten the two wheel supports to the underside of the fuselage assembly.

10. Install each wheel by slipping it onto a 5/8" wire nail and then driving the nail into one end of a support so that the nail is located 1/4" from the support's bottom edge. Don't drive the nail in all the way; leave a 1/16" clearance between the end of the support and the inside face of each wheel.

11. Finish the Space Cruiser any way that you like. The project in the photograph was detailed with latex enamel paints.

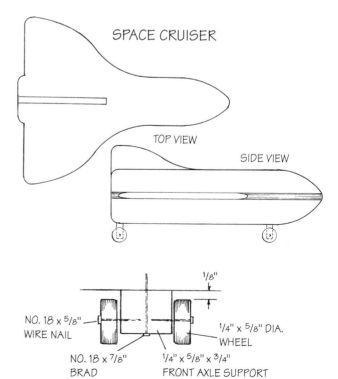

SPACE CRUISER

TOP VIEW

SIDE VIEW

1/8"

NO. 18 x 5/8"
WIRE NAIL

1/4" x 5/8" DIA.
WHEEL

NO. 18 x 7/8"
BRAD

1/4" x 5/8" x 3/4"
FRONT AXLE SUPPORT

WIND ROLLER
●●●●

A gentle breeze is all the power you'll need to start this fascinating featherweight rolling. For thrilling races, build Wind Rollers in sets of two or more!

CUT LIST

2 Top and bottom • 1/8" x 2-3/4" x 8-1/2"
2 Sides • 1/8" x 1/2" x 8-1/2"
1 Mast support • 1/2" x 3/4" x 6-1/4"
4 Wheels (see "Tips") • 1/8" x 2-5/8"-diameter
4 Axle supports • 1/2" x 1/2" x 1/2"
2 Axles • 1/8" x 6" dowel
1 Mast • 1/8" x 10-1/2" dowel
1 Boom • 1/8" x 8" dowel
1 Sail support • 1/8" x 11" dowel
1 Mast-tube plug • 1/4" x 1/2" dowel
1 Flag-tube plug • 1/8" x 1/2" dowel

HARDWARE AND SUPPLIES

2 No. 17 x 5/8" wire nails
1 3d finishing nail
1 7/32" x 10-3/8" aluminum tube (Mast tube)
4 7/32" x 1-1/4" aluminum tube (Axle-spacer tubes)
1 5/32" x 1-1/4" aluminum tube (Flag tube)
1 10" x 10" piece of aluminum foil
1 1-1/4" x 4" piece of heavy paper
1 6" length of braided string

SUGGESTED TOOLS

Layout tools
Claw hammer
3/8" drill
1/16", 1/8", and
  5/32" twist-drill bits
Scissors

TIPS

- *This unique wheel-and-axle arrangement is designed especially for the Wind Roller's balsa-wood construction.*

- *The mast-tube and flag-tube plugs are trimmed to fit inside their respective tubes.*

- *The wooden parts, which are made from balsa wood, are available at craft stores, as are dowels, aluminum tubing, and braided string.*

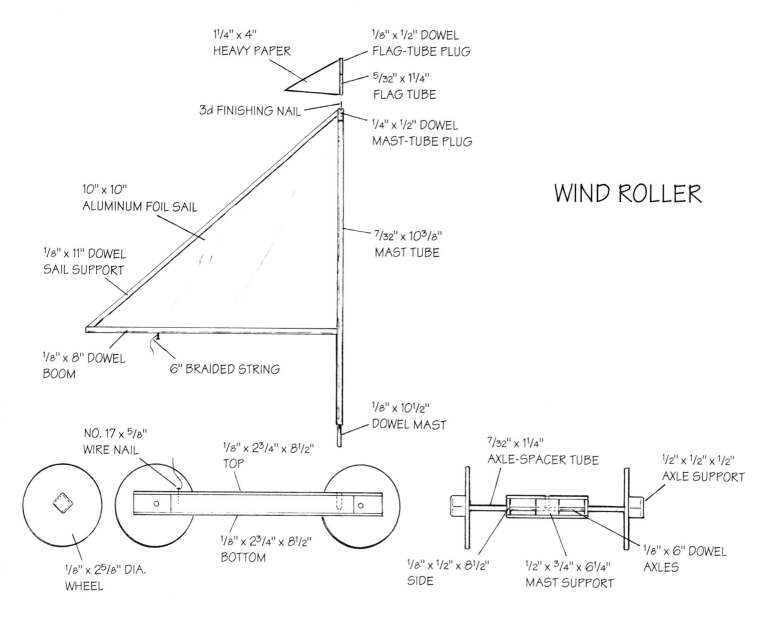

1¼" x 4"
HEAVY PAPER

⅛" x ½" DOWEL
FLAG-TUBE PLUG

5/32" x 1¼"
FLAG TUBE

3d FINISHING NAIL

¼" x ½" DOWEL
MAST-TUBE PLUG

10" x 10"
ALUMINUM FOIL SAIL

7/32" x 10⅜"
MAST TUBE

WIND ROLLER

⅛" x 11" DOWEL
SAIL SUPPORT

⅛" x 8" DOWEL
BOOM

6" BRAIDED STRING

⅛" x 10½"
DOWEL MAST

NO. 17 x ⅝"
WIRE NAIL

⅛" x 2¾" x 8½"
TOP

7/32" x 1¼"
AXLE-SPACER TUBE

½" x ½" x ½"
AXLE SUPPORT

⅛" x 2¾" x 8½"
BOTTOM

⅛" x 2⅝" DIA.
WHEEL

⅛" x ½" x 8½"
SIDE

½" x ¾" x 6¼"
MAST SUPPORT

⅛" x 6" DOWEL
AXLES

INSTRUCTIONS

1. After laying out the flat wooden parts, place them on a smooth surface such as plywood and carefully cut them to size, using a utility knife with a sharp new blade.

2. Run a line of glue along one 3/4" edge of the mast support and place that edge onto one face of the bottom piece, centering its length along the length of the bottom and locating one end 1" from an end of the bottom piece. (This is the front end of the assembly.)

3. Glue one edge of each side piece onto the same surface of the bottom.

4. Glue the top piece onto the assembly in identical fashion to the bottom piece, squaring everything up carefully before gently clamping the assembly together.

5. Through the top of the assembly, bore a 1/8" mast hole, 1/2" deep, centering it across the assembly's width and locating it 1-1/2" from the front end.

6. To accommodate the axles, bore a pair of centered 5/32" holes on each side piece, locating each hole 3/4" from an end.

7. Lay out and cut to length the dowel pieces and the aluminum tubing parts. (Sever the latter by rolling your utility knife gently across them.)

8. Use a bit of glue to install the mast in the mast hole.

9. Lay out a mark on the top piece, centered 1-1/2" from the rear of the assembly. Tap in a wire nail at that point, leaving 1/8" of the nail length projecting from the assembly's top surface. This is the support to which the boom will tied.

10. Using your center finder, locate the center of each wheel. Then form a cross shape by marking two perpendicular lines through the center. Glue an axle support onto each wheel's face, using the lines to center each support in position.

11. Locate the center of the unmarked face of each wheel and bore a 1/8" hole, 3/8" deep, into each point. The wood is paper-light, so easy does it with your drill!

12. Lightly sand all wooden parts. Also use fine sandpaper to smooth any sharp ends on the aluminum tubing.

13. Glue one end of each axle into a wheel's axle hole. Slide an axle-spacer tube onto the free end of each axle. Then slide each axle through a pair of matched holes in the base assembly and slip a second spacer onto its free end. Finish by gluing a second wheel onto each axle's end.

14. Cut the aluminum-foil sail in the shape of a right triangle. Its two 8-1/2" edges should meet at a 90-degree angle; its third edge forms the 12-1/6" hypotenuse.

15. The sail assembly is made up of a mast tube, boom, sail support, and sail; its "leg" is formed by the end of the aluminum mast tube. Rest the sail flat on your work surface and run a thin line of glue around its perimeter, placing the glue line about 1/8" inside the sail's edges. Set the mast tube onto the glue line, aligning one end with the point where the hypotenuse meets one 8-1/2" edge, and carefully roll the gluey foil around the tube.

16. Position one end of the boom against the mast tube so that a 3" length of mast tube projects below the sail. Roll the gluey foil around the boom.

17. Set the sail support onto the last gluey edge so that its ends connect the two ends of the boom and mast; then roll the foil edge around the sail support. Secure the three corners by placing a large drop of glue where the dowels and tubes meet. Let the assembly dry thoroughly.

18. Whittle the mast-tube plug with your utility knife until it fits into the top end of the mast tube. Then install it with a drop or two of glue so that its end is flush with the tube's end.

19. When the glue has dried, bore a 1/16" hole, 3/8" deep, in the plug's center.

20. Gently tap a 3d finishing nail into the hole, allowing a bit of the head to protrude.

21. Whittle the flag-tube plug until it fits the flag tube and install it into the flag tube in a manner similar to that used in Step 18.

22. Fold the paper flag in half across its length and then cut it across its diagonal. Unfold the flag, apply glue to one side, and fold the flag in half around the flag tube so that the flag's 90-degree angle is located nearest the open end of the tube. Press the gluey sides together to secure the flag in place.

23. Bore a 1/16" hole through the boom, locating it 2-1/2" from the end farthest from the mast tube. Gently tap a wire nail into the hole, leaving 3/8" of nail projecting from the hole.

24. Set the mast tube onto the mast and the flag tube onto the finishing nail above it.

25. Tie the ends of the braided cord to the two wire nails. Detail the project with latex enamel paints and protect the unpainted wood with varnish. The project in the photo was painted with a racy-looking number in bright colors. For protection against the elements, give your Wind Roller a couple of coats of water-based satin varnish. A bit of wind and a smooth, level surface will provide your child with hours of racing fun!

METRIC CONVERSION CHARTS

VOLUMES

1 fluid ounce	29.6 ml
1 pint	473 ml
1 quart	946 ml
1 gallon (128 fl. oz.)	3.785 l

WEIGHTS

0.035 ounces	1 gram
1 ounce	28.35 grams
1 pound	453.6 grams

LINEAR MEASUREMENTS

INCHES	CM	INCHES	CM
1/8	0.3	20	50.8
1/4	0.6	21	53.3
3/8	1.0	22	55.9
1/2	1.3	23	58.4
5/8	1.6	24	61.0
3/4	1.9	25	63.5
7/8	2.2	26	66.0
1	2.5	27	68.6
1-1/4	3.2	28	71.1
1-1/2	3.8	29	73.7
1-3/4	4.4	30	76.2
2	5.1	31	78.7
2-1/2	6.4	32	81.3
3	7.6	33	83.8
3-1/2	8.9	34	86.4
4	10.2	35	88.9
4-1/2	11.4	36	91.4
5	12.7	37	94.0
6	15.2	38	96.5
7	17.8	39	99.1
8	20.3	40	101.6
9	22.9	41	104.1
10	25.4	42	106.7
11	27.9	43	109.2
12	30.5	44	111.8
13	33.0	45	114.3
14	35.6	46	116.8
15	38.1	47	119.4
16	40.6	48	121.9
17	43.2	49	124.5
18	45.7	50	127.0
19	48.3		

ACKNOWLEDGEMENTS

I'd like to thank the following people, businesses, and organizations for their generous contributions to **Wood on Wheels***:*

ANNE KELLEY MCGUIRE,
   psychoeducational therapist, for advice on developmentally appropriate play and for critiquing the projects

MARGARET ANNE MULDER KELLEY,
   for project suggestions and for her sewing skills

ROGER AND PAT MCGUIRE,
   for project suggestions

TERESSA MUCKLEVENE,
   for assistance with our younger models

STEVE HOLLADAY,
   (Holladay Paint & Wallpaper, Asheville, NC) for technical advice on finishing the projects

EVAN BRACKEN,
   for his outstanding photography

DON OSBY,
   for his excellent illustrations

ASHEVILLE URBAN TRAIL, ASHEVILLE, NC,
   for the photography location pictured on pages 122, 126, 130, and 132

CITIZEN'S HOME CENTER, ASHEVILLE, NC,
   for technical advice on the projects

The best of the mountains in one place,
CHIMNEY ROCK PARK,
   P.O. Box 39, Chimney Rock, North Carolina, 28720, for allowing me to reproduce the photo on page 72

Thanks, too, to
MARY RITTER,
   (Group Sales/Public Relations at Chimney Rock Park) for having located these photos

KING-THOMASSON ANTIQUES, INC.,
   Asheville, North Carolina, for permitting us to photograph their antique toys (page 116)

JOANNA WILLIAMS,
   professor of Art History at the University of California, Berkeley, for allowing me to reproduce her photograph (page 78) of wood toys made in Sonepur, India. This photo is from the San Francisco Craft & Folk Art Museum exhibit entitled "The Monkey With the Flaming Tail—Lanka Podi Festival of Sonepur, India."

FRIENDS AND FAMILY,
   for their enthusiastic support and for providing locations for photography

THE KIDS,
   who test-drove the projects, and their adult helpers

JOHN FAHERTY,
   whose expert hands are shown on page 25

OUR FEARLESS MODELS

David Shalom Birnham

Sara Devin Clark

Olivia Kieffer

Marika Le Lapham

Kayla Lindsey

Molly McGuire

Kelly Olesiuk

Sarah Olesiuk

Kendral Presha

David Rudow

Ian Barton Simpson

Ariana Weaver

Jessamyn Weis

Karla Weis

Asher Williams

Dylan Williams

Joseph Williams

INDEX